CO-ASY-795

WHAT'S IT WORTH?

*Probing Our Values With
Questions Jesus Asked*

COVER DESIGN
by
Cynthia Euing Cox

WHAT'S IT WORTH?

Probing Our Values With
Questions Jesus Asked

Margaret Ragland

P.O. BOX 1060

QUALITY PUBLICATIONS

ABILENE, TEXAS 79604

© Margaret Ragland 1977

All rights reserved. No part of this publication may be reproduced, stored in a retrieval system, or transmitted in any form or by any means electronic, mechanical, photocopy, recording, or otherwise, without prior permission of the copyright owner.

ISBN: 0-89137-409-4

Unless otherwise specified, all scriptural quotations are from the Revised Standard Version, and used by permission.

Excerpts from LIVING ZESTFULLY. Written and Copyright renewal 1959 by Clovis Chappell. By permission of Abingdon Press.

Excerpts from QUESTIONS JESUS ASKED by Clovis Chappell. Copyright renewal 1976 by Clovis Chappell, Jr. By permission of Abingdon Press.

Excerpts from SERMONS ON SIMON PETER. Written and Copyright renewal 1959 by Clovis Chappell. By permission of Abingdon Press.

Excerpts from THE SALTY TANG by Frederick B. Speakman are Copyright 1954 by Fleming H. Revell Company. Used by permission.

Excerpts from ANYONE FOR CALVARY by Charles Ray Goff are Copyright 1958 by Fleming H. Revell Company.

TABLE OF CONTENTS

FOREWORD

Dear Readers,

These lessons were originated to fulfill a need among the women of our own congregation for an in-depth study to promote a sense of God in everyday life—one which would permeate our every action. Those who participated in this effort spent many hours in research, study, thought and soul-searching. It is our desire to pass on to you the benefit of these hours.

We are greatly indebted to such men as William Barclay, Batsell Barrett Baxter, Clovis Chappell, C. S. Lewis, Francis Schaeffer, and to such women as Catherine Marshall, Eugenia Price and Helen Young. We have quoted freely from these writers, not that we accept them as authority on spiritual matters, but that their words so beautifully and adequately express what we believe to be Bible truth. Bible quotations abound also, and in most instances the Revised Standard Version is used.

And now may I introduce our guest writers. All are devoted Christians, wives, and mothers, and members of the Meadowbrook Church of Christ at the time of origination of these lessons.

Mrs. Jim Claunch (Betty) is the mother of three boys, and is a Bible teacher of juniors and of teenage girls.

Mrs. Earl Lawson (Shirlee), mother of four daughters and one son, was for many years a beloved pre-school teacher, writing some of her own material. More recently, she has been involved in teaching Bible at a group home for teenage girls who are estranged from their families.

Mrs. Tom Reaves (Gayle), a devoted homemaker, has one son and one daughter. Along with her husband, who is a deacon, she is actively involved in the work of the church.

Mrs. William Robertson (Carol) has three sons, one daughter and three grandchildren. She has served as coordinator of the Primary

Bible School Department and is presently teaching third grade level.

Mrs. C. P. Seabrook (Inez) has three grown sons and four grandchildren. Both she and her late husband, who served as an elder for many years, have instructed and inspired Christians through their excellent Bible teaching.

Mrs. Tom Sibley (Sandy), a minister's wife and a young mother of three, is a very effective speaker and teacher.

Mrs. David Thomas (Jan) is the wife of a young doctor and the mother of two small children. An excellent school teacher, she is presently retired to devote herself to the rearing of her young family.

To these dear sisters in Christ we are indebted for their cooperation in this effort. In addition, this work is an expression of deep gratitude and love to my husband, who, as a dedicated Christian and church leader, a devoted husband and father, has inspired and encouraged me through the years.

Will you accept this study course in the love with which it is intended; and wherever it is weak or inadequate, let your own Bible knowledge fill in the gaps.

—Margaret Long Ragland

LESSON 1:
Cost vs. Value In Today's Market
(an Introduction)

LESSON SCRIPTURE: **"Do you want to be healed?"**
John 5:1-9
OTHER SCRIPTURES: 2 Corinthians 13:5   Matthew 11:16-19
Philippians 1:9, 10   Matthew 23
Luke 15:2

Erma Bombeck has a gift with her satire of picturing everyday incidents (right down there where you and I live) in such a ridiculous way that it is extremely real and hilariously funny at the same time.

In a recent newspaper column, she said that she went to the grocery and spent $52.34 and when the boy who bagged the groceries and carried them to the car asked her where she wanted them, she said, "I have some other errands—just put it in the glove compartment." She said, "Really, this grocery buying has become ridiculous! Why I can remember when my station wagon runneth over with $52.34 worth of groceries, and now I can't even afford help for my hamburger!" You know, she made a valid point because she said one thing this situation has done; it has made us stop and evaluate. She said, "I have some friends who at night used to put a banana and cereal in the baby's crib and sleep the next morning. Now, at 85¢ a box, we want to know what that cereal is going to do!"

And so we have come to say: WHAT DOES IT COST—and WHAT IS IT WORTH?

I know you, like I, have stood and seen women at the store (not only that, but been there yourself), with the ad out of the paper and all the little coupons clipped and hunting for every bargain you could find. So I think we have become extremely conscious about what things cost and what they are really worth. This is not, of course, just in the line of groceries, because it faces us everywhere. We see it on the news and in things we pick up. Just this past week in one of my bills there was a letter which said: "As a retail specialty shop we have become somewhat concerned with the apparent state of our economy, just as you too are probably concerned. We think it time to state several things to you which we consider very important—things about price, quality and service."

So our world today, I think, is very conscious of this sort of thing, so much so that I wonder some times if we don't see and hear too much of it—if we aren't just too conscious of it, and maybe if we aren't too concerned. I am not suggesting that the state of the economy is not a serious thing, because it is a grave problem especially in some sections of our country where many people are out of work. As I write this, our nation is in the midst of an economic trauma, experiencing at once recession and inflation, whopping profits for some industries and sharply rising un-employment for others. With apparent abandon, some people are engaging in wild buying of luxury items, while, among the wage-earners, anxiety is becoming widespread. Even though the situation is serious, it is not the most important value with which we should be concerned.

Maybe we need to be a little more concerned with the true values, and maybe we need to evaluate ourselves and our values and be concerned with some things that are lasting and really matter. In a time in which our dollar is being devaluated in the money market, maybe we need to devaluate its importance in our own minds. Maybe we need to do some *devaluating* and some re-evaluating. Maybe we need to examine ourselves and ask ourselves some questions:

Just what are my values, and how do my actions show them?

What do my children, my husband and my friends see in me that shows what I consider valuable?

What value do they see me place on material things?

Can they tell by my example that God is important in my day to day living?

Do they see in me a peace of the presence of Jesus?

Do they see me as seeking approval from peers or from God?

Do they see me as a minister of love?

Do I inspire my children to right living by my own life?

"Examine yourselves, to see whether you are holding to your faith. Test yourselves. Do you not realize that Jesus Christ is in you?—unless indeed you fail to meet the test!" (2 Corinthians 13:5).

This course is designed to make you *THINK*! Think about your values; think about what they cost God; think about what the cost is to you in terms of discipleship; think about how you live your values. We are going to the teachings of Jesus as a basis for this study—to some of the many probing questions which he asked. And, as we reflect on the questions of Jesus and attempt to relate

His teachings to our present situation, other questions will present themselves. You are urged, as you follow this study, to seek honest, sincere and scriptural answers.

Before we start a study of specific values, I want to throw out some things for you to begin thinking about. You know, we find ourselves today having been influenced through the years by all our experiences and by people with whom we come in contact.

What has determined the values you have?

What are the things that affect us and help us to decide what our values are?

Probably one of the greatest influences is the home that we grew up in, our training, what we saw in our mothers and fathers. There was a survey made some time back by a denominational group among college students. One of the things that showed up in this survey was that how religious or faithful to his religion a child is depended a great deal upon the religion of the mother—not what she was, but what the child *thought* she was. This certainly points up the fact that our children are influenced by what they *see* in us. I am not so much concerned about whether you and I love our children and are striving to teach and train them. The thing I am most concerned about is if they see in us a God that is real and if they see by our example that our love for them is a love coming from God, and if they see a love and respect of parents one for the other. I have come to believe that one of the greatest things we can give our children is that they can see demonstrated a genuine love for God and a love and respect between parents.

Our home has also influenced what we believe about God's Word, and surely our values are established to a large degree on the understanding we have of God's love and His law. "Understanding" is a key word, for the proper assessment of values depends on constant study and search for wisdom and understanding, rather than acceptance of superficial and "pat" answers.

As we grew up, the thinking of our peers had a great deal to do with what we considered valuable. This peer pressure is strongest during the teen years, a time when many important decisions are made. We are aware of this fact with our children and we try to be very careful who their friends are, but sometimes we lose sight of it as we grow older. Whomever we do associate with—we influence them and they us, no matter how old or how young we are.

What else influences our values? Would you say that the time in which we live, the accepted social behavior, the economic condition, the state of prosperity in which we find ourselves—all of this would help determine values? Certainly, circumstances change from time to time; and we, consciously or unconsciously, absorb some of the philosophy and mores of our culture.

Catherine Marshall, in *Beyond Ourselves,* has a description of a time she calls the "Optimistic Era," when the values for which Americans were searching lay in the material world, with inner values taking second place. The cure for the pain and evil of the world was to be found in human institutions and in better environmental conditions. The ideal was to be a nice, tolerant person, avoiding religious creeds and dogma, having an attitude of live and let live. This was the *American Way.*

Catherine Marshall concludes by saying, "So we believed. So we acted."[1]

What is the American Way today?

When you think of the expression "THE AMERICAN WAY OF LIFE", what image comes to your mind?

Happy-Go-Lucky?

Two cars in the garage?

Freedom—of speech and choice?

People working and making their own life?

What other image comes to your mind?

Do you think we would be considered as middle class Americans? As far as the entire world is concerned, those who read this book are probably above middle class in education and economic status. But, looking only at the United States, most of us would be considered middle class. Have you ever stopped to think that, as middle class Americans, we have absorbed certain values?

There was a very thought-provoking article by Craig Watts in a magazine called MISSION in which he talked about middle class values. He said, "Do we dare claim, as some people do, that Middle America has been so influenced by Christianity that their values are very similar to the values and standards of Christ? If we accept the interpretation of Christianity that many have, we fail to see any extreme difference between the nice person clinging to middle class values and the Christian."

Then, going on to explain what he means by middle class values: "Central to the middle class value is the belief that a balance is best. This surgical balance is the striving for the mean between the various opposites in extremes that arise in our life. In the middle of the road one does not have to worry about being far out on a limb alone. Never will he stray far from the herd."[2] We want to be like the rest. This is the middle class value of *balance*; and he said growing out of this are two others that are very close, and they are *respectability* and *security*. Most other middle class values are in some way related to them. It often seems that the motto is "What will people think?" and this expression has been used by so many people to ease their children into the mold of the masses, that sometimes children growing up in Christian homes are unable to distinguish the difference in what people think and what God wants. Respectability and Christianity seem to just melt into one. We must watch what we say, what we do, what we wear, and above all, watch to make sure we associate with the right people. Public approval is the goal of the middle class man and he will do very little to upset his standing before others. But—greater than this, is the value of safety, because we prize nothing greater than our own selves and those who belong to us. And so our own security must be prized at all cost and must be saved at all cost.

"And so together stand the three: balance, respectability, and security; the trinity of the middle class. Here is the foundation of the nice, normal life."

Is anything wrong with normal middle class values? What does Christ have to say to this?

"A life ruled by middle class values can best be described by one word: 'mediocre.' It is a life that flickers and never really blazes. The intensity of life that can be found in the extremes of Christ is sacrificed for a superficial contentment.

"The call of Christ beats against balance. He never tried to pretend that His call was reasonable or practical by any worldly standards. Christ's emphasis of a radical call drove many away. Jesus' desire for balance could not be more absent than His desire for respectability. His most scalding condemnations were reserved for the good acceptable religious people of His day (Matthew 23). He never sought the right people to associate with (Luke 15:2). He neglected to censor the actions and words of the 'good people' around Him who referred to Him as a glutton and a drunkard (Matthew 11:19).

"Those who believe Christ wants us to live good, normal lives have never really heard His call at all. The middle class values and their fruit of mediocrity must crumble at His call, and our very existence must be a protest against the ordinary."[3]

Do you see your Christianity as "mediocre"? Are you willing to look at yourself objectively and recognize your values for what they are? And are you willing to say, with the author of *The Salty Tang*:

"We who have made a cult of pace, we who complain of these hurried, hectic days, and yet are perversely a little proud of it all and like to wear our busyness as a badge—we must, somehow, give a new hearing to Jesus' insistence that redemption, abundant living, great living if you will, is really a matter of emphasis, a question of priorities, a matter of selection."[4]

This is what this course is all about!

DO YOU WANT TO BE HEALED?

This question Jesus asked of a man 38 years old, crippled from birth, in an incident at the pool of Bethzatha, recorded in John 5:1-9. According to William Barclay's commentary, the word for pool used here comes from the Greek word which means "to dive," indicating that it was a deep pool. "Beneath the pool there was a subterranean stream, and every now and again the stream bubbled up and disturbed the waters of the pool. In Revised Standard, verse 4 is left out, which explains that an angel came at certain seasons to trouble the water, and those who got in were healed. The reason for this is that most of the older and better manuscripts left this out; thus most scholars think that some scribes later added the explanation. Anyway, this was a very common belief in Jesus' day and so the man is believing in the belief of the day."[5]

But Jesus came to him and said, "Do you want to be healed?" Why do you think He asked him this? Wasn't it very evident that the poor man did want to be healed? Why do you think Jesus asked him this question?

Have you ever been ill or recuperating from something and have someone say to you, "Do you really want to get well, to get out and get going?"—or tell you that someone else had the same thing and is out by now! It is true that some people enjoy poor health, leaving all the work, worry and responsibilities to someone else. Some are complacent in the acceptance of their condition; others accept what must be, and move on to new vistas of living. Regardless of one's outlook, it is rather irritating to be asked if you really *want* to get well.

Perhaps Jesus posed the question in order to get the man's attention. Don't you imagine that all eyes would focus immediately on one who would ask such a thing of any of those pitiable creatures around the pool? Whether we realize it or not, Jesus is constantly trying to get our attention, trying to get us to listen, to focus on Him. Whatever the reason, Jesus did ask him this question and we know the rest of the story. He went on to tell the man: "Get up! Pick up your bed! Walk!" The man could have said, "I can't do that." But, instead, he made the effort and with Jesus' help— with the two of them together, the man trying and Jesus furnishing the power—the healing took place.

Today Jesus comes to us and says to us, "Do you want to be healed? Do you want to be changed?" You know, we really have to want a thing for it to happen. This world is not going to be Christian until we have a burning desire for it. And we are not going to desire it until we are totally committed ourselves. We can say, "Do unto others as you would have others do unto you," but we are not going to do this until we love—genuinely love—our neighbor, and we are not going to love our neighbor until we really and truly love God. And we will not really and truly love God until we learn to live with Him each day. We can quote "Man's life consists not in the abundance of the things he possesses", but as long as we are busy possessing, nobody is going to listen to us.

And so we have to *want* to be healed—we have to want to be whole—and I feel that maybe Jesus is looking at us and He is saying: "Do you want to be totally committed? Do you sincerely want to be a Christian?" He's saying, "I see you trying to be Christian, trying to live Christian lives, but I see you merely existing, crippled all your life by a less than perfect value system. The fact that you can't get up and walk and run in the mainstream of life and be joyous and happy and enjoy this abundant living and all the glorious blessings that I have for you is because you have not wholeheartedly embraced the marvelous values that I have held up to you. Some of the values to which you are still holding fast need to be re-examined. Do you really want to be healed?"

"My prayer for you is that you may have still more love—a love that is full of knowledge and wise insight. I want you to be able always *to recognize the highest and the best*, and to live sincere and blameless lives until the day of Christ."[6]

FOR CLASS DISCUSSION:

Many questions have been raised in this lesson. We suggest you discuss further those that are most pertinent to the needs of your class.

FOOTNOTES:

1. Catherine Marshall, *Beyond Ourselves* (Old Tappan, NJ: Spire Books), p. 21.
2. Craig M. Watts, "Christian Commitment and Middle Class Medocrity," *Mission,* June 1974.
3. Watts.
4. Frederick B. Speakman, *The Salty Tang* (Old Tappan, NJ: Fleming H. Revell Co., 1954), p. 32.
5. William Barclay, *The Gospel of John, Vol. I* (Philadelphia: Westminster Press), pp. 172-173.
6. Phillippians 1:9-10 The New Testament in Modern English, Rev. Edn., by J.B. Phillips 1958, 1960, 1972. The Macmillan Co., New York, NY.

LESSON 2:
Cost of Discipleship

LESSON SCRIPTURE: ". . . first sit down and count the cost?" Luke 14:28
OTHER SCRIPTURES:
Luke 14:25-33
Matthew 16:24-26

As we gathered in the auditorium on Wednesday night for a short devotional service, a young man stepped out of his pew and strode confidently down the aisle in response to the song of invitation. Gary, the youth minister, took his confession, asking, "Do you believe that Jesus is the Son of God? Are you willing to dedicate your life to Him?" This young man made the good confession and as he went up to be baptized, down the side aisle came marching at least four or five of our teenage boys, smiling, going up to be with George as he became a Christian. When George and Gary went into the water of the baptistry, again Gary asked if he was willing to make Jesus the lord of his life. And there he was baptized into Christ and rose to be a new person. As we prayed for George, we were enveloped in the beauty and solemnity of the occasion. I did not know George personally, but, for some time he had been attending classes and worship, enjoying fellowship with our young people, studying and learning about Jesus. I don't know what kind of person he is; I don't know what kind of life he has lived. But I do know this: whatever he was before this time, when he arose from the waters of baptism he was a new person; he was reborn; everything that was behind him was completely forgiven; he was white as snow, with life new and fresh before him. Now, as you read about George, just suppose that to you this were a completely new concept. Wonder what your reaction would be? Do you think you would say, "That is the most marvelous thing I ever heard. That's the most wonderful possession that anyone could have, to have everything behind him, gone completely, and a new and fresh start in life!"

17

Do you think you would say, "I want that above anything else. That must be the most precious possession a person could own. That must be the costliest thing a person could buy; and if I have enough money—if I have enough to buy it—that's what I want. How much is it?"

I would say, "No, you can't buy it; you don't have enough money to buy it. You don't have enough of anything to buy it, but God offers it to you because He bought it for you. He has already paid the greatest price that has ever been paid, and so it is yours— free, if you accept it."

And you would say, "How do I accept it?"

The answer: "Do like George did. Believe that Jesus is the Son of God, and confess Him, repent of your sins and confess them, then put on Christ in baptism. Obey your Lord as He has asked you to do, and this possession will be yours."

And you might say, "But surely there is something that He asks of me; there is some price that I must pay for such a wonderful gift."

And suppose I say to you, "Well, yes, after that you must observe the Lord's Day; you must worship; you must partake of the Lord's Supper; you must give of your money; and you must attend the services of His church. There are things that you must *not* do: Don't lie; don't cheat, steal, commit adultery, and so on. There are also things you *do*: do good works."

Would you agree that what I have enumerated is the cost of discipleship? Check each item—do these certain things and don't do certain things. Is this the price tag that you and I consider that God has placed on His gift of new life?

May I emphatically say *no*, that's not it, not it at all! But don't misunderstand! Although these are commands to be obeyed and, therefore, are very important, they are not the *cost* to us—they are *privileges*.

"The Lord's Day is my tower of strength. It is the day of days for soul refreshment. In moments of quiet meditation I have often asked myself, 'How long will strength remain in me and God's reality remain in my heart, if it were not for the soul renewing worship of the Lord's Day?' How wise our Heavenly Father was to provide this day for His children! It is a time that He has planned for spiritual food for my hungry soul."[1]

The Lord's Day and the worship, the Lord's Supper, even giving some of what God has given us—this is one of our blessings. He certainly expects us to give our money, but not in payment for discipleship. Is attending the different services of the church a chore to you—a cost—or is it a blessing? What about assembling with fellow Christians and admonishing one another? Do you feel that coming together as a family and getting strength from each other is a privilege? Do you consider each moment of worship as a renewal of spirit, a continuing rebirth?

What about DON'T, DON'T and DON'T—and DO, DO, DO? Now again, don't misunderstand! As we go beyond the gospels and Christ's teaching, we find the many letters that have been provided for us in God's Word (and thank God we do have them). They tell us of actions that are pleasing to God and also those that are not. But don't you know some people that observe many of these "don'ts" and "do's," who do good works, but who are not Christians, who don't even claim to be Christian? So surely this is not our cost. This is *some* of the outward manifestation of what it means to be a Christian.

It may be that, at the time we put on our Lord in baptism, very few of us realize fully the true cost of discipleship as given in the words of Jesus in Luke 14. Who understands what it means to hate one's own family? Who is willing to deny self totally? Consider what Jesus says in Luke 14:25-33.

> Now great multitudes accompanied him; and he turned and said to them, "If any one comes to me and does not hate his own father and mother and wife and children and brothers and sisters, yes, and even his own life, he cannot be my disciple. Whoever does not bear his own cross and come after me, cannot be my disciple. For which of you, desiring to build a tower, does not first sit down and count the cost, whether he has enough to complete it? Otherwise, when he has laid a foundation, and is not able to finish, all who see it begin to mock him, saying, 'This man began to build, and was not able to finish.'

> "Or what king, going to encounter another king in war, will not sit down first and take counsel whether he is able with ten thousand to meet him who comes against him with twenty thousand? And if not, while the other is yet a great way off, he sends an embassy and asks terms of peace. So therefore, whoever of you does not renounce all that he has cannot be my disciple."

Now, first of all, in verse 25 Jesus said if you are going to be my disciple, you must hate your family. Some translators have used *"love me more"* instead of "hate." Love me more than mother, father, husband (instead of wife as we are looking at it from the woman's viewpoint) child, sister, brother, even your own life. Thus, hate in this passage would mean putting God ahead of all others, even those loved ones you hold so dear. We couldn't study through the Scriptures and get the idea that God wants us to hate our family, for this would be incongruous with His other instructions to love and provide for our own. So Jesus says, "You must love Me more than all of your loved ones." Is this a problem for us—to love God more than our own family?

In a study group, the fact that in heaven there will be no marriage or giving in marriage was being discussed and one young woman spoke up and said, "That's hard for me to accept because the love my husband and I have for each other is so deep that I just don't like to think about heaven or think about a place where we wouldn't have this love between us." It is easy, from a human viewpoint, to think this way; but to do so is to lose sight of the promise that in heaven we will live in God's love—a love so much greater than any kind of love relationship that we enjoy on this earth. Perhaps the reason He said hate your family was that He knew that our family— those so close to us—naturally are the ones we love the most. So He is saying, "Love *Me* more." How can we do this? Isn't the secret to be found in loving your family *through* God, rather than love reaching out to each other on a lateral basis, letting your love go upward to God and back? A family united in love for God will find not only that their love for each other is sweeter, but that putting God first comes more naturally.

This ideal situation, however, does not always exist. Many families are not united in Christ, and there are Christian women who are faced with the problem of a marriage partner who has little regard for God's way and His word. How does a woman, in this situation, love God more than her husband and still obey His command to be in subjection to her husband? Such a woman should study carefully 1 Corinthians 7:12-16 and 1 Peter 3:1-6. In applying these Scriptures, and evaluating her own situation, surely she will find consolation in the words of James: "If any of you lacks wisdom, let him ask God, who gives to all men generously and without reproaching, and it will be given him" (James 1:5).

We know the people to whom Jesus was talking in this passage were faced, more so than we are today, with the fact that, if they accepted Christ, they renounced their families. They also had to prove, by their willingness to die, that they *loved God more than life itself.* When Jesus spoke these words to His disciples, He knew what persecution they were facing and that they were destined, almost to a man, to be martyred. We aren't called upon to suffer such extreme persecution today; and yet when you come right down to it, if we face life with the constant goal of safety, security, comfort and ease, and all our decisions are made from a worldlywise and prudential motive, it may be that we miss not only all life is about here but in the hereafter too. "Life becomes a soft and flabby thing when it might have been an adventure. Life becomes a selfish thing when it might have been radiant with service. Life becomes an earthbound thing when it might have been forever reaching for the stars. The man who risks all—and maybe looks as if he had lost all—for Christ finds life. It is the simple lesson of all history that it has always been the adventurous souls who bade farewell to security and safety who wrote their names on history and who greatly helped the world of men."[2]

If there hadn't been men who were willing to take risks, we wouldn't have some of the medical skills we have today; and if there hadn't been those who were willing to take risks, we wouldn't have many, many of the machines and conveniences that we have today. And if there had not been women who were willing to take risks, none of the children would be born. After you and I take this sort of risk to bring children into the world, then how far do we go in lavishing upon them ease and comfort and seeking for them this goal of safety and security rather than one of adventure, one that would lead upward?

To use a very mundane illustration, when our children were teenagers, my husband wanted us to spend one Christmas together at a ski resort. Knowing little about snow skiing, I was afraid, and never agreed to go. Since our children have grown and left home, the two of us have enjoyed a few days at a ski resort. It was then that I realized he had been right, for the children would have loved it. We could have given them memories of lofty, snow-covered grandeur, crisp mountain air, tired bodies relaxing happily by a huge log fire. Now as they are grown and away from us, when they come home they have had many new experiences, but they like to talk about the things that we did together. Because of my lack of adventure and my hanging on to the goals of safety and security, I didn't give to them these memories, and now it is too late. I'm sure there were also opportunities of much more lasting value which we passed up.

Mothers, build memories for your children! Build spiritual memories—enjoying together the natural beauties of our world, helping a needy family, going on campaigns for Christ, bringing joy to an elderly person—anything you can do together to bring you closer to God.

To get anywhere for Jesus we have to make sacrifices and take some risks. If there hadn't been people willing to launch out, take a few risks, and give up a little comfort and ease, would we have today the ghetto ministries, halfway houses, foreign missions—even behind the Iron Curtain? Would we have the chance to influence the lives of people in those situations? Too many of us want to hang on to the comfort of the life we now enjoy, when what we need is to launch out. You know, when you look at the Scriptures, you don't see God very concerned about the ease and comfort of his saints. Reading in the Old Testament, we are amazed at the things they dared for Him. Even though God gave them many of the material things to enjoy, we don't see Him concerned for their security or comfort. Even Jesus, when He was about to be crucified, prayed the prayer in the garden for His disciples, for those who had followed Him and whom He loved so much, saying, "Father, I don't ask that you take them out of the world, I ask that You keep them from the Evil One." In this prayer we see Him concerned not for their safety, but for their character. Perhaps Jesus is not asking of you and me a day, or a week or a year, but He is asking for our whole life. In the busy pace of life today, we need to stop and think just what this means. We need to "count the cost."

"Which of you desiring to build a tower, does not first sit down and count the cost." He must reckon just how much it is going to cost, before he starts to build, because if he can build only the foundation and cannot complete the structure, he will be laughed at. Surely the main concern of Jesus here is not that his disciples would be laughed at but that they follow Him with a real awareness of what it means—of what the cost will be and of what it will take to endure. The endurance is further emphasized as He calls their attention to a king going to war. Will he not first consider whether he can win with the amount of soldiers that he has; and, if not, will he not attempt to make peace? Is Jesus admonishing us to realize what this discipleship is going to cost in resources? Is He urging us to seek the source of strength if we see we do not have what it takes? We have just said that He wants our whole life. He is asking us to deny ourselves completely. The cost is my whole self; it involves the necessity of complete inward surrender of everything for the love of Christ.

The acts of obedience mentioned earlier in this lesson, as well as the "do's" and "don'ts," are like outward veneer unless they come from something inside. If· they are a manifestation of inner spiritual strength, then they are something that will endure. If we have fought our battles within, then when the trial comes, it is much easier to overcome. Looking inward, if you see that all you can build is the foundation, then unless you are willing to come to grips with the fact that God is going to be the ruling influence in your life, then you can't finish the tower. If you are a king going to battle with an army of your own resources, take stock of what your own resources are. With your resources alone, can you endure? With mine—no. And that's why I must come to God and say, "Give me of Your person, take over and You rule my life, God, with me making myself available and giving myself to You in complete obedience." This is the cost—my complete self, my self-will, everything about me given up to God, so that He may give me a new self, one born from above.

As our bodies, hearts, and minds become His to control, it is then we can say "no" to self and "yes" to God. When we obliterate self as the ruling principle of life and make God the ruling principle, then and only then have we understood the meaning of Jesus' words in Matthew 16:24: "Deny himself" (RSV), "leave self behind" (NEB), "give up all right to himself" (Phillips), "forget himself" (TEV).

Why is it so hard to deny self? What is this self, anyway? Each of us is tinctured with self-will, with self-ambition, with the desire to be pampered and admired, with overcriticalness of others and oversensitivity to ourselves, with a desire to inflate our ego with the accumulation of things.[3] All of this is what we would call the *selfish me*, and it is there in every one of us (some aspects of it more in some than in others). Although we try to keep the good self forward, that other self keeps cropping up. Remember what Paul said? "The things that I want to do, I don't do . . ." he said, realizing this problem that our human self-will and selfishness often overrule us. Now one consolation is, if I understand my Bible right, that when I became a Christian, I became a new creature. My helplessness against sin has been remedied because I have Christ living in me. This does not mean that I sin no more, but that the blood of Jesus Christ continues to cleanse me; and as I yield my self-will to Him, sin no longer rules my life. Each day I will still have to choose between self-will and God's will, but the big decision to let Christ rule makes each daily decision easier.

The need for *daily* self-discipline cannot be emphasized too strongly. We know that the spirit is willing but the flesh is weak; we are, therefore, admonished to "watch and pray." Regular daily prayer is a great help, as is daily meditation on the Word of God.

To begin each day with the right "mind-set" is a very valuable tool. We read in Romans, "those who live according to the flesh set their minds on the things of the flesh, but those who live according to the Spirit set their minds on the things of the Spirit." Our minds are powerful indeed, and the right mind-set can influence the entire day. When you wake up in the morning all your thoughts come at you like animals—your activities and your desires and plans for that day come rushing at you. Just push them back for a moment, take that other attitude and listen to that other voice; come away from some of your fussing and fretting and let that larger, stronger and quieter life come flowing into you.[4] Start the morning with your mind thinking, "Today I live for God and I am open." It is true that when you have set your mind in this way, sometimes you look back on that day and realize that a special opportunity in living for the Lord was presented to you. You may find that on the days you are able to deny self and put God first, everything else seems to fall in place.

It is an exhilarating thought that when we exchange this self-will for God's will, it is then that we discover the true self. The more we get what we now call "ourselves" out of the way, the more truly ourselves we become. What I so proudly call "myself" is only an accumulation of my heredity and upbringing, my surroundings and my own desires. Even my desires often spring from my physical organisms or from ideas I have gotten from other people. The more I try to "be myself" without Christ, the more I try to live on my own self-will, the more I become dominated by my own heredity and upbringing and surroundings and desires; but when I exchange this self-will for God's will, I find a greater strength, a finer quality of character, a more useful personality.[5]

FOR SUCH A DISCOVERY OF ONE'S TRUE SELF, CAN ANY PRICE BE TOO HIGH?

FOR FURTHER STUDY AND DISCUSSION:

1. If we answer the call to discipleship, what decisions and partings will it demand? Will it lead to a division between our lives as workers in the world and our lives as Christians?
2. When the early disciples were called, they literally left *all* to follow Christ. Are we called upon to do just that today? Why or why not?
3. Discuss what discipleship means specifically for the homemaker, the worker, the business woman.

FOOTNOTES:

1. James LeFan, "The Lord's Day Brings Renewal," *Christian Woman,* April 1969, p. 3.
2. William Barclay, *The Gospel of Matthew, Vol. 2.* (Philadelphia: Westminster Press), pp. 168-169.
3. Catherine Marshall, *Beyond Ourselves,* (Old Tappan, NJ: Spire Books), p. 189.
4. C.S. Lewis, *Mere Christianity* (New York: MacMillan Publishing Co., 1943, 1945, 1952), p. 165.
5. C.S. Lewis, *Beyond Personality* (New York: MacMillan Co.) p. 67.

LESSON 3:
Price Of The Cross

"Was it not necessary that Christ should suffer these things?" Luke 24:26

LESSON SCRIPTURE: Luke 24:25-27
OTHER SCRIPTURES: Ephesians 2:8-10   Psalm 22:16-18
Galatians 6:14   Isaiah 53:4-11
Hebrews 10:1-11   Jeremiah 33:14-18

"The Alamo is *not* for sale!" booms a Texan in reply to the joke about the rich Arab attempting to buy the Texas shrine for his son. We smile at such jest, but perhaps we look with a little less humor on the reports that the oil-rich foreigners are buying huge chunks of stock in our large American corporations. It is a matter of concern that on the international scene our diplomats are groping with the problem of the world's wealth trickling to the oil countries where, if this continues, the over balance of wealth will be concentrated. It boggles the mind to think of the possibility of the vast wealth of the world gradually concentrating itself in one place, such as the country of Iran, for example. In that country I understand that the Shah has very great influence—could the Shah of Iran end up with all the world's resources? What kind of figure would that be—all the wealth in all the world? It staggers the imagination! And yet we know that if this one person, or any one person, had that much wealth they still could not buy their soul's salvation.

Today's newspaper, which devotes a large amount of space to the problems of the price of oil and the balance of wealth, also runs a cartoon depicting a human body dumped in the garbage can with the caption, *The Only Thing That Is Getting Cheaper Is Human Lives.* And yet God says this life, because of the soul that lives within it, is very precious. It's more precious than all the wealth that it is possible to accumulate.

25

If the vast wealth of the world piled up in one place is a staggering thought, and we agree that one soul is much more valuable, how can my finite mind even begin to place a value on the cross on which God sacrificed the life of His Son to pay the price of redemption of all mankind?

If I could be the Shah, if I could be this person who has all the wealth in all the world, I think I could give that up quicker than I could sacrifice the life of either one of my sons. We are told that a person might lay down his life for a friend, and I might (I don't know if I could) be able to sacrifice my own life if it were necessary. But I don't believe I could ever willingly and deliberately sacrifice the life of one of my sons. This helps us understand something of the price of the cross, as far as human sacrifice is concerned. And yet, as far as the cost to God in the sacrifice of His Son, and as far as the cost to Jesus Christ, it may be beyond our power to comprehend. But, thank God, we do not have to understand it nor have the answers to all the questions in order to reap the benefits.

However, there are many questions which are asked in the Bible and we want to examine some of them to try to see more clearly the meaning and the price of the cross. In Luke 24:26, Jesus raised one question when he said, "Was it not necessary?" In this incident the time is the first day of the week after the crucifixion, the day on which the Lord arose. Two of his disciples were walking along the road to Emmaus, which is about seven miles from Jerusalem, and they were discussing the things that had happened as Jesus joined himself to them. "What is all this that you are talking about?" asked Jesus. Not recognizing Him, they replied, "Surely you must be the only man in Jerusalem who does not know what has happened. This prophet, Jesus Christ, who was mighty in works and deeds, has been crucified; and we thought surely he was the prophet who had come to save Israel. Not only that, but this morning some of the women have gone to the tomb, and they report that his body is not there." At first Jesus rebukes them, saying: "O foolish men and slow of heart to believe all the prophets have spoken! Was it not necessary that the Christ should suffer these things and enter into his glory?"

Even though rebuking them, it seems that Jesus offered some consolation by saying, "Was it not necessary?" If we see something unpleasant as being *necessary,* we can accept it a little better; whereas, if we feel something is completely unnecessary, we find it very difficult. Consider, for instance, an automobile accident in which lives are lost. When we learn that a drunken driver is the cause of that accident, we immediately think, "Oh! that was so unnecessary. How tragic!" On the other hand, when we see someone with a terminal illness and no hope for recovery, it is easier for us to accept death.

It seems, also, that Jesus looked at the cross as necessary in light of all that the prophets had foretold. You remember the time that Jesus asked, "Whom do men say the Son of man is? . . . Whom do you say that I am?" and Peter replied with that great confession that he was the Christ, the Son of God. The following paragraph in that chapter (Matthew 16) reads: "From that time Jesus began to show his disciples that he must go to Jerusalem and suffer many things . . . and be killed, and on the third day be raised." Peter immediately said, "God forbid, Lord! This shall never happen to you." Jesus replied, "Get behind me, Satan! You are a hindrance to me; for you are not on the side of God, but of men." Then again, on the night on which Jesus was betrayed, when the soldiers came to the garden to take him, Peter pulled out his sword in defense. And again, Jesus rebuked Peter, saying: "Do you think that I cannot appeal to my Father, and he will at once send me more than twelve legions of angels? But how then should the scriptures be fulfilled, that it must be so?" (Matthew 26:53-54). Thus we see that Jesus looked upon the cross not as a tragic misfortune, but as a necessity.

Several times Jesus mentioned the necessary fact of fulfilling Scriptures. In fact, all through his ministry he alluded to it. You remember that he said, "Think not that I have come to abolish the law . . . ; I have come not to abolish (it) but to fulfill (it)" (Matthew 5:17). Granting, then, that Jesus did look on the cross as necessary, the question comes to mind: WHY WAS THE CROSS NECESSARY?

Was it to fulfill Scripture? In our lesson Scripture we are told that he began with the prophets and related to them the things that had been said, concerning him. Have you ever made a study of the many prophecies concerning Jesus? The list would be very long. We might think specifically of the 22nd Psalm, which begins with the words of Jesus on the cross, "My God, my God, why hast thou forsaken me?" This psalm also contains such descriptive passages as "They pierced my hands and feet . . . They divided my garments among them, and for my raiment they cast lots." Isaiah 53 is a classic passage about Christ:

> Surely he has borne our griefs and carried our sorrows; yet we esteemed him stricken, smitten by God, and afflicted. But he was wounded for our transgressions, he was bruised for our iniquities; upon him was the chastisement that made us whole, and with his stripes we are healed. All we like sheep have gone astray; we have turned every one to his own way; and the Lord has laid on him the iniquity of us all.

We can see in these sad words a description of the crucifixion.

Was Jesus crucified in order that he might fulfill the Scriptures? Was that the reason? Did he have to suffer this particular kind of death in order to fulfill the Scripture?

Let us consider some facts. Christ shed his blood for our salvation. In doing so, he did fulfill Scripture and fulfill the law; but the reason for his death was to redeem sinful mankind. That was God's purpose; that was what He sent Jesus to do. God, in his foreknowledge, knew the need for a means of salvation for sinful man; thus, the cross was planned from the beginning. The Scriptures were written because this was the way the plan would unfold—not that these events took place because that was the way the Scriptures were written. It was not that Christ had to fit into the mold, so to speak, but rather that God inspired the prophets to speak the things that were to come to pass. And let us never forget that it was because of his great love for mankind that He made his plan.

Consequently, when Christ came into the world he said:
'Sacrifices and offerings thou hast not desired, but a body hast thou prepared for me;
in burnt offerings and sin offerings thou hast taken no pleasure.
Then I said, 'Lo, I Have come to do thy will, O God,'
as it is written of me in the roll of the book' (Hebrews 10:5-7).

Hebrews 10 gives us a very clear picture of the plight of man under the old law: man could not keep the law perfectly, and the blood of bulls and goats could not take away sin. No sin can be with God; thus, one has to be sinless in order to live with him eternally. Just suppose that for *one day* I could live perfectly (and I know that is impossible). But, even supposing that I could be sinless for one day, my goodness for that day would not make up for what I did yesterday, nor would there be any left over to cover my imperfections on the morrow. You can see, then, that even if it were possible for me to live perfectly one day, I am still in a terrible plight, because it is impossible for any human to live perfectly day after day. This being the condition man was in under the old law, God saw the cross as the way to reconcile man unto himself. When Jesus came to earth and became a man, then that human nature that suffers and dies was amalgamated with God in one person. This person could help us. He could suffer and die, because He was human, and He could do it perfectly, because He was God. You and I could accomplish such a feat only if God does it in us. Jesus Christ could do it only if He became a man.

This human and divine combination is the thing that is hard for our finite minds to comprehend; it raises questions to which man alone cannot find answers, and some will not accept the answers that God's word gives. For instance, even in my own experience, there was a time when I found it very difficult to see what was so special about Jesus' death on the cross. (I'm sure a mature Christian will find this rather naive, but this type of thinking may be a problem for one with less knowledge and understanding.) When I would hear people discussing the great sacrifice that Jesus made in his death on the cross—how terrible and cruel it was—it occurred to me that other men in history have been martyrs, others have died just as cruel a death. In fact, there have been human beings on this earth who, from a human standpoint, may have suffered more; because the ordeal of Jesus lasted only a matter of hours, whereas there have been those who were tortured (in all sorts of cruel and inhumane ways) for days, even weeks and months.

I finally became aware of the fact that the error in my thinking was the expression "from a human standpoint." Jesus was not only human, He was God, and as He hung there on the cross, He bore the guilt of every creature who ever lived or ever will live. Anyone who has experienced a deep sense of guilt knows how devastating and how agonizing it is. Can you even imagine what it would be like? He gave up everything willingly, and He bore all my guilt, all your guilt, and that of everyone who lived before, now, and in the years to come.

There are, also, people who say, "If Jesus were God, then the crucifixion loses all its value, because it would have been so easy. God can do anything." True because "with God all things are possible." Not only could God perform the sacrifice easily, He could do it perfectly. Only the sacrifice of perfection can help us. If Jesus had been *only* human and imperfect, would his death have helped us?

"The perfect submission, the perfect suffering, the perfect death, were not only easier to Jesus because he was God, but were possible only because He was God. But surely this is a very odd reason for not accepting them? The teacher is able to form the letters for the child because the teacher is grown-up and knows how to write. That, of course, makes it easier for the teacher; and only because it is easier for him can he help the child. If it rejected him because 'it's easy for grown-ups' and waited to learn writing from another child who could not write itself (and so had no 'unfair advantage') it would not learn very quickly."[1]

Jesus could make the perfect sacrifice because He was God and He could suffer because He was man. You and I, also, are both human and divine (of course, not in the same sense that Jesus was). But we have a human body and we have an immortal soul which has come from God and which longs to go back to God. At the cross, then, we can see man at his wicked worst, but we can also see man as a creature of infinite worth. In the cross we see a love that will not let us go—a demonstration of the words of Jesus, "And I, when I am lifted up from the earth, will draw all men to myself."

"I think there are many who call themselves Christian who still regard Calvary as the world's most desolate hill. But if we reject it thus, we lay bare our ignorance of the Christian faith and all for which it stands. When we really understand this faith, we understand Calvary and we know it is not awful but awe-full, full of awe, and we stand amazed in its presence. It is the divine event that holds man and the world together; it is deep calling unto deep, the haunting strains ennobling something from beyond that call to the deepest within us. And so I see more on Calvary's hill than just a man being killed, more than an execution or a death. I see in it something more than the work of man at his worst, something more than a crowd of people intent on killing a man, something more than a throng rejoicing that they had him at last, something more than a taunting mob crying, 'Why don't you save yourself?', something more than a pitiful body hanging there between the earth and the sky.

"Calvary? Oh, that is something to sing about! It has given birth to some of our finest music. It pulls at the heart of mankind. Looking down through life, man sees not death and bitter winter, but hope and fellowship and love. Here is revealed a love that will not let us go!"[2]

Here is revealed God's love in the glorious gift of His grace. It is like removing the final wrappings of a long awaited and promised gift and revealing its priceless contents. Consider carefully the following:

"But God, who is rich in mercy, out of the great love with which he loved us, even when we were dead through our trespasses, made us alive together with Christ (by GRACE you have been saved), and raised us up with him, and made us sit with him in the heavenly places in Christ Jesus, that in the coming ages he might show the immeasurable riches of his GRACE in kindness toward us in Christ Jesus. For by GRACE you have been saved through faith; and this is not your own doing, it is the gift of God—not because of works, lest any man should boast. For we are his workmanship, created in Christ Jesus for good works, which God prepared beforehand, that we should walk in them" (Ephesians 2:4-10, author's emphasis).

"Since all have sinned and fall short of the glory of God, they are justified by his GRACE as a gift, through the redemption which is in Christ Jesus, whom God put forward as an expiation by his blood, to be received by faith . . . (Romans 3:23-25, author's emphasis).

Grace is a word that cannot appear too often in our Christian vocabulary; yet, it seems to me, that through the years we have not emphasized it enough in the Lord's church. Oh, we define it. "Grace is unmerited favor," we say. "Grace is God giving Himself for us in this loving way." But very seldom, in my experience, have we studied its meaning in depth; too few sermons have been focused on the grace of God. It seems that we have taken this grace and placed it where we can admire it from a distance—as if to say, "This is a priceless gem, and we will put it back here for

..eping; then once in awhile we will take it out, dust it off, and ..dmire it.'' Our dialogue is more often centered around our own responsibilities toward salvation: that is, obedience to God's commands. But joyously, every day, we should be wearing this pearl of great price—the fact that Jesus died and bought for us the salvation of our sins.

At the Abilene Christian University Lectureship in 1973, the late Dr. Roberts (who was at that time head of the Bible Department at ACU) conducted three class sessions on the subject of justification by grace, based on the teachings of Paul in the book of Romans. The son of a preacher, Dr. Roberts said he started going to gospel meetings with his father as a small boy, always sitting on the front row. Although constantly exposed to preaching, as he grew into adulthood and became a preacher and teacher himself, he began to realize that he could not remember hearing a sermon on the subject of grace.

Some of the reason for such a lack surely lies in the reaction of well-meaning Christians to religious error concerning grace that grew out of the Reformation. At that time, there were those who contended that since salvation comes by the grace of God, there is, therefore, nothing a person can do or has to do. "Grace alone does everything," they said. "Let not the Christian attempt to erect a new religion of the letter by endeavoring to live a life of obedience to the commandments of Jesus Christ! The world has been justified by grace!" That was the heresy of the enthusiasts, the Anabaptists and their kind. The followers of Martin Luther made the same mistake, embracing this cheap grace, misunderstanding that to Luther grace was very costly. After Luther left the monastery, his study led him to grasp by faith the free and unconditional forgiveness of all his sins. That experience taught him that this grace had cost him his very life, and must continue to cost him the same price day by day. When he spoke of grace, he implied as a corollary that it cost him a life of obedience. Luther had said that grace alone can save; his followers took up his doctrine and repeated it word for word. But they left out its invariable corollary, the obligation of discipleship, of obedience to Christ.[3]

Then our Christian fathers, in reacting to the mistake of such a cheap grace, stressed the importance of obedience to Christ, to the extent that sometimes grace seemed to be minimized. As Dr. Roberts suggested, we seemed to be afraid to dwell on the subject for fear we would be misunderstood and placed in the category of the error mentioned above. Such classes on grace as Dr. Roberts was teaching are an indication that Christians today have renewed interest in the subject.

Then let us leave such fears behind, rejoicing in our salvation through the free gift of God's grace, realizing that this grace is so costly that it demands my all, my life devoted to Him, my complete obedience to Christ.

"Such grace is *costly* because it calls us to follow, and it is *grace* because it calls us to follow *Jesus Christ*. It is costly because it costs man his life, and it is grace because it gives a man the only true life. It is costly because it condemns sin, and grace because it justifies the sinner. Above all, it is *costly* because it cost God the life of his Son: 'ye were bought at a price', and what has cost God much cannot be cheap for us. Above all, it is *grace* because God did not reckon his Son too dear a price to pay for our life, but delivered him up for us. Costly grace is the Incarnation of God.

"Happy are the simple followers of Jesus Christ who have been overcome by his grace, and are able to sing the praises of the all-sufficient grace of Christ with humbleness of heart. Happy are they who know that discipleship simply means the life which springs from grace, and that grace simply means discipleship."[4]

One young woman has suggested that if this concept of grace had been fully taught her as a teenager it might have saved her a lot of damaging guilt feelings, as there were times when she thought of herself as so bad that she could never get forgiveness, no matter what she did. She felt that if the hope that God's grace promises had been presented to her in the right way, the despair she felt at the time could have been overcome with joy and renewed zeal.

"It was like opening a door to me," said another, relating how she had been a Christian about ten years when she heard a sermon on grace, delivered by Otis Gatewood.

"I had heard of grace, but my understanding at that time was of a kind of grace that you had only as long as you were good. If you did something wrong, then you didn't have it anymore. If you were a Christian, your past sins were forgiven; but if you sinned again, you were right back in the same boat as before. But Brother Gatewood explained how in grace one is sanctified, and the blood of Christ *continues* to cleanse from sin. It is not that one is justified in deliberately sinning, but he is saved as long as he is making an effort to do his best and is daily asking forgiveness through prayer. Christ's blood is daily cleansing from sin, and there is no need for guilt feelings for a Christian who is really trying."

And this makes the Christian life joyous! We should be singing His praises *every day* and expressing gratitude to Him for His willingness to suffer so for us. The price of the cross is immeasurable, and we should luxuriate in reaping its glorious benefits. But, in our exhilaration, let us not forget the price He calls upon us to pay. Let us remember that we are called upon to suffer *with* Him, to share the burden of the cross, and to take up the cross daily. The sure word of our Lord is that every one who would follow Jesus *must* take up his cross.

What does this mean? How can we suffer with Him? What does it mean to take up one's cross?

As Jesus hung there on the cross, what human experiences did he undergo? To name a few: pain, agony, rejection, humiliation, ridicule, death. Jesus, the suffering servant, is also the rejected Son of God. The cross means rejection and shame as well as suffering. One meaning of the Cross, for us, must be to SHARE THE SUFFERING OF CHRIST to the fullest. But how do I do this? How can I share the suffering of Christ?

It is true that some of us experience more suffering than others in this life. Sometimes this suffering can rightly be labeled "suffering for Christ." Sometimes it can be attributed only to our own wrong-doing, negligence or misjudgment. Sometimes it is our lot because of circumstances beyond our control. Often we tend to look upon such burdens as "our cross to bear," but does the cross of which Jesus is speaking mean even more than this?

Do you remember that once Jesus said, ". . . as you did it to one of the least of these my brethren, you did it to me," and that Christians are admonished to bear one another's burdens? Jesus, who need never have suffered at all, deliberately asked for pain and anguish and for guilt—*our* guilt! In doing so, He showed the cross to represent an understanding fellowship—the fellowship of the troubled. One way to suffer with Christ is to share the suffering of others, going through the deep valley with those in woe. "Taking up one's cross thus represents understanding and insight into human trouble and fellowship with kindred hearts."[5]

These kindred hearts are to be found everywhere, for trouble lies hidden in the heart of those you pass on the street, sit beside on the bus or plane, or share a friendly cup of coffee with. Sometimes this fellowship of suffering demands your time, energy, even emotional anguish. Other times just to be an interested listener suffices, or to offer an earnest and sincere prayer.

Basically, the cross means sacrifice; to take up one's cross also means to take up the BURDEN OF SACRIFICE. The cross stood for sacrificial living as well as sacrificial dying. We are prone to quote Romans 12:1 and 2, "present your bodies as a living sacrifice, holy and acceptable to God . . ."; but though quoted often, seldom is this passage applied with the power intended. Too often, presenting our bodies as a living sacrifice has been limited to religious activities, whereas the Christian life is also the life of sacrificial service.

How long has it been since you or I did any work for God that caused us actual pain or discomfort or sacrifice? How long will we be satisfied to give only that which is easiest to give—a little money, a worn garment, a can of beans? How often are we willing to take the time to give our Christian discipleship the personal touch?

"The Christian may have to abandon personal ambition to serve Christ; it may be that he will discover that the place where he can render the greatest service is somewhere where the reward will be small and where the prestige will be non-existent. He will certainly have to sacrifice time and leisure and pleasure in order to serve God through the service of his fellow men. To put it quite simply, the comfort of the fireside, the pleasure of the visit to a place of entertainment, may well have to be sacrificed for the duties of the eldership, the calls of the youth club, the visit to the home of some sad and lonely soul. He may well have to sacrifice certain things he could well afford to possess in order to give more away. The Christian life is the sacrificial life.''[6]

To take up one's cross, then, means to take on the dedicated life. To bear the burden of the cross means to bear the burden of sacrifice and suffering. There is a lovely paradox here! This same Jesus who said that in order to be his disciple we must take up the cross also comes to us, saying, "My yoke is easy and my burden is light."

"We have a tendency to gasp with amazement when we hear Jesus say, 'My yoke is easy.' What was his yoke? It was the yoke of a perfectly dedicated life. It was a yoke that made his life one long toil up Calvary. Yet he tells us that the yoke that cost him so much was kindly. This was certainly true. In spite of the cross, yes, and because of the cross, Jesus lived more richly, more joyously, I take it, than any other man that ever set foot upon this planet. The abundant life that Jesus lived he shares with his followers.''[7]

The abundant life is the life of sacrifice and service, and it is both hard and easy. It may be hard to hand over the self to Christ, to sacrifice human desires and selfish interests, but it is far easier than what we are trying to do. For, so often, we find ourselves trying to keep our heart and mind centered on money or ambition or pleasure and to be morally good, honest, humble and loving at the same time. To be pulled in two directions is frustration and misery—a hard life. To lose our lives in sacrifice and service is to find the abundant life—the yoke that is easy.

"The command of Jesus is hard, unutterably hard, for those who try to resist it. But for those who willingly submit, the yoke is easy, and the burden is light. Only the man who follows Jesus single-mindedly, and unresistingly lets his yoke rest upon him, finds his burden easy, and under its gentle pressure receives the power to persevere in the right way.''[8]

FOR FURTHER STUDY AND DISCUSSION:

1. Recommended outside reading for this lesson is Chapter Two on "Costly Grace" of Dietrich Bonhoeffer's *Cost of Discipleship*. Discuss this reading along with Ephesians 2:4-10.

2. Discuss the areas of sacrificial service open to Christian women today.
3. Share with each other ideas of the greatest needs in times of anxiety and trouble and the services each has found to be most helpful.
4. Have someone give a report to the class on Bishop's *The Day Christ Died*.

FOOTNOTES:

1. C.S. Lewis *(Mere Christianity* (New York: MacMillan Publishing Co., 1943, 1945, 1952), p. 58.
2. Charles Ray Goff, *Anyone for Calvary?* (Old Tappan, NJ: Fleming H. Revell Co., 1958), pp. 41-43.
3. Dietrich Bonhoeffer, *Cost of Discipleship* (New York: SCM Press Ltd., 1959), p. 53.
4. Bonhoeffer, pp. 47-48, 60.
5. Goff, p. 35.
6. William Barclay, *The Gospel of Matthew, Vol. 2* (Philadelphia: Westminster Press), p. 167.
7. Clovis Chappell, *Questions Jesus Asked* (Nashville: Abingdon Press, renewal 1976), p. 20.
8. Bonhoeffer, p. 40.

LESSON 4:
Knowing God Personally

**"He who has seen me has seen the Father; how
can you say, 'show us the Father'?"** John 14:9

LESSON SCRIPTURE: John 14:9-10
OTHER SCRIPTURES: John 1:18   Psalm 4:4
                        Colossians 1:15, 19   Psalm 46:10
                        John 17:3   Isaiah 55:8-9
                        2 Peter 1:2-3   Jeremiah 31:33, 34

The Bible is respected as a book about God, even by those who
deny its inspiration or who do not profess faith in God. To
Christians it is an inexhaustible source of knowledge, instruction
and spiritual strength—a message from God. It's all inclusive,
opening with the words "in the beginning" and closing with a vision
of the New Jerusalem, the eternal city.

Here is a book which reveals not only God, but also man in his
relationship to God. In the opening chapter, we read that God
created the universe, the earth and all its plants and creatures. His
final creation was man, Adam, to whom he gave dominion of all
creation. Reading on into Genesis, "beginnings," the fifth chapter
tells us, "This is the book of the generations of Adam." Adam's
genealogy consists of a repetition of statements of "so-and-so" lived
so many years, begat "so-and-so," and died.

"The whole story seems to be this: There is a little row of cradles
over here, a little bunch of coffins over there. A handful of petty
people are climbing out of the cradles, walking a few perfectly
futile steps, then toppling over into the coffins. That is all there is to
it. But just as we are preparing to leave off reading out of sheer
boredom, we come upon this exquisite bit: *'Enoch walked with God.'*

"What happened to Enoch? For a while, life meant no more to
him than his fellows. He merely existed. Then one day, because he
had a deep yearning for God, the hand of God, that is always

feeling for our weak hands, found the groping hand of Enoch and drew him into fellowship with himself. Enoch became acquainted with God, and it came to pass that the whole meaning of life for this man could be put in this single sentence, 'Enoch walked with God.'

"Now if Enoch succeeded in making contact with the Great Friend in that far-off day, certainly such a high achievement ought to be possible for you and me. We have so much better opportunity! Since then, great saints have entered into this experience and given us the benefit of their findings.''[1] Better still, Jesus himself has come to show us God.

What does it mean to walk with God? Can I walk with God today?

To walk with God must mean to be ever under His eye and to feel that He is constantly near. To walk with God means to make His Word our rule and His glory our goal in every action, to comply with His will, to concur with His designs. To walk with God is to live a life of communion with Him, not only in prayer, but also in daily living, to be workers together with Him.

Now I say all this; you listen, and you say, "That is well and good. I want to walk with God in that way, and I wish I could. But life is so complicated today. I have these children to look after and care for—these runny noses to wipe. I have the house to clean, the clothes to wash, the grocery shopping to do, the errands to run, the carpools to drive. I have this part time job to fulfill in addition to all the work at home. Later on, when I get older and things settle down to a simpler routine, then I can walk with God as you describe. But, right now, it is too difficult."

Let us remind ourselves that life doesn't work that way; for, whatever we are going to be, we are becoming that kind of person today. Someone has said, "Don't marvel that God does such great things, but marvel that He stoops to do such little things." It is my opinion that walking with God also means wiping those runny noses, looking after that family, and rubbing elbows with the world—wherever our paths take us. Walking with God means to combine whatever we are doing in life with fellowship with God—to have God always near and very real to us.

I am concerned about our feeling that God is a real personality and having this secure base to come back to, no matter what happens. I am concerned that we give such a security to our children, and let them see that God is a very personal God to us. We cannot be saved for our children, but we can give them a security so that when they have matured and they look back, they can say, "To my mother, God was very real. She walked with God." This is one priceless gift you need to give your children.

Then how can I walk with God? What is of value in attempting to know Him personally? Let us assess this value from various viewpoints.

1. In order for us to know God and for Him to be very real to us, how much do we need to UNDERSTAND Him? Do we need to understand His ways and His thoughts? Do we need an answer to every question?

"For as the heavens are higher than the earth, so are my ways higher than your ways and my thoughts than your thoughts" (Isaiah 55:9). We must realize that our finite minds can comprehend just so far; we must not try to fit God into a human mold or make him meet our standards. We need to realize that even beyond our wildest imaginations is God's power, His wisdom and His love.

In the book of Job, we see that Job's friends are sure that they understand why God has so allowed Job to be inflicted; whereas, having read the first of the book, we know that the so-called friends do *not* understand. The knowledge which they think they have has made them puffed up and intolerant at a time when they need to be loving and sympathetic. We can look at the discoveries of science and we can be in awe of the accomplishments in space. But we still need to be in awe of the God who "laid the foundation of the earth" and "shut in the sea with doors." Even though our spacemen have gone to the moon, satisfactorily completed a link-up with the Russians and are now looking toward Mars for future landings, God can still say to them and to all of us as He did to Job, "Where were you when I made the stars?"

In order to feel that we really know God, there are some things about Him that we do not have to understand. Does God give us understanding of what we need to know? "The secret things belong to the Lord our God; but the things that are revealed belong to us and to our children forever, that we may do all the words of this law" (Deuteronomy 29:29). Surely God has revealed to us what He knows that we can comprehend; need we trouble ourselves about the many unrevealed things which we cannot comprehend? Remember, He has given us "all things that pertain to life and godliness. . ." (2 Peter 1:3). All things that we need to know, as far as our salvation is concerned, and for knowing God and loving God, have been given unto us.

2. Is it of value to study and know ABOUT God?

This seems like a foolish question, for surely any sincere believer realizes the value of learning about God. We start our little children in Bible school in the cradle roll, teaching infants about God and the love of God. We are constantly studying about God all along life's journey. And yet no knowledge *about* God can take the place of *knowing God*. Theology is a respected science, but theology is studying about God, not knowing Him personally. I could be an expert on bread, knowing all about its food value and caloric content, being able to make a variety of breads. But if I don't eat it, it will never satisfy my hunger. The delicious smell of homemade bread baking in the oven is better than reading about it, but it does not compare with the experience of tasting a slice of the hot bread with butter melting on it. That's the real thing!

The real thing is knowing God—not just knowing about Him!

I may know all about water, but my tongue will become swollen, my lips parched and my body wracked with pain if I have no water to drink. Knowledge about water will not suffice—neither will knowledge about God without knowing God.[2]

3. But thanks be to God! He has SHOWN US A WAY to really know Him! When Phillip said in John 14:8, "Show us the father," he was breathing a prayer that has been on the lips of men all through the ages—*show* us, not tell us about, but *show* us God. A demonstration, an object lesson, an example, makes an abstraction understandable; for it is not clear to us until we see it in terms of something that is real to us. God remains an abstraction until we see Him in terms of personality. For instance, if you are trying to explain "light" to someone, you might go to the dictionary for the definition. But that would not be worth nearly as much toward understanding what light is as would be one glimpse of a glowworm or a firefly. In like manner, the dictionary definition of "life" is so dull one would hardly want to live if that were all he knew about life. The definition of God is the same way. Everything we learn *about* God helps us to know who He is, but none of the information we may gather is sufficient to *really know* Him.

In thinking of all the things we see Jesus doing, and the characteristics and attributes he reveals, we come to know God, the Father. We see Jesus having an intimacy with God, talking often with Him in prayer. We see Jesus acting as if there is no doubt that his necessities will be provided. We see Jesus concerned for bodies as well as souls. We see Jesus showing the Father as being all-loving and forgiving. We see Jesus indignant at injustice, hypocrisy and greed. We see Jesus keeping the law, faithfully. We see Jesus as all-knowing, seeing into the hearts of men, understanding their problems, compassionate in their suffering. We see Jesus as all-powerful—healing the sick, raising the dead, calming the storm. We see Jesus showing no partiality, but reaching out to all strata of society, showing empathy to all with whom He comes in contact.

Someone has suggested that in Jesus we cannot see the *whole* of God, since He was limited by time and by space and by dwelling in a human body. And yet is there anything about God that He does not reveal, except His omnipresence? "The Son is the radiance of God's glory and the exact representation of his being" (Hebrews 1:3 NIV). "He is the image of the invisible God, the firstborn of all creation; for in Him all things were created, in heaven and on earth, visible and invisible . . . . He is before all things, and in him all things hold together . . . . *For in him all the fullness of God was pleased to dwell"* (Colossians 1:15-19). Even though limited by time and space and perhaps the customs of the day, surely Jesus reveals to us the whole of the character and attibutes of God. "He who has seen me has seen the Father."

4. Even though Jesus is the ultimate revelation of God, let us not overlook any source in our search to know Him. What is the value of seeing God in the NATURAL UNIVERSE? Can we know Him through the wonders of the creation? We start teaching our children at a very early age about God's world because it is something that they can see and understand. As adults, the beauties of nature are something that we, also, can see and appreciate. One way that we can partially realize God's love for us is by truly loving His creation, for "the earth is full of the steadfast love of the Lord" (Psalm 33:5).

"We try to count the stars or to touch a cloud and we appreciate God's magnitude. We hear music in raindrops and we know God's harmony. We pause at the song of a bird or the flutter of a butterfly and they remind us of God. Tears flood our eyes as we behold God's glorious sunset, a lump comes in our throat as we stand beneath a California redwood, an unexplained swelling fills our breast as we view a forest in its fall splendor."[3] On a lovely spring morning, as we behold the fresh green of the trees, a myriad of color in a flower garden, dewdrops sparkling on young, tender blades of grass, our spirits are lifted upward and we cry, "Surely, only God could design such beauty. Did He not put something of Himself into His creation?"

In the area in which I live, we are blessed with a beautiful countryside. Here I can look at nature and proclaim, "God is a wonderful artist!" But what if I lived in Siberia, or the desert or some other desolate place? We must admit that there are some very ugly and very frightening things about our world. Longfellow, the poet, penned this observation: "The laws of nature are just, but terrible. There is no weak mercy in them. Cause and consequence are inseparable and inevitable. The elements have no forbearance. The fire burns, the water drowns, the air consumes, the earth buries." But even here we can see God's dependability. It would, indeed, be a frightening thing to never know if water would quench fire or burn itself!

It is true that some of us may not be able to see the beauty in the barrenness of the desert; yet we know that God made all things good in His sight with a purpose for each creation. Have we not seen in recent years that when we trifle with the balance of nature the results can be drastic? When we complain about bad weather, we should be reminded that all weather occurs for a purpose. "Is not this our Father's world, and does not He know what is best for it? Think how clear the air is after a storm. The rain quenches the thirst of dry crops. A hurricane may cause property damage, but does not one make us aware of how temporal our earthly possessions are? This might be one way God has of keeping us humble."[4] Both God's power and His wisdom are demonstrated in the physical elements.

"Talk ye of all His marvellous works," said the psalmist (Psalms 105:2 ASV). The wonders of nature lie all about us, patiently waiting for us to view them, to enjoy them, to comment on them. We should be thankful for them and take pleasure in them, for there is a value in seeing God in nature that we must not overlook. Time spent in viewing God's creation with and through the eyes of our children is invaluable. But let us never make the mistake of stopping there, for if we teach them to see God in nature only and do not lead them to see Him in Jesus Christ, we have robbed them of the value of actually knowing God. Christ is a solid rock, a friend to turn to amid doubts or disaster. If one knows God in nature only, when calamities come his way he has nothing of reality to steady him.

There are those who seek to go beyond the natural to the psychic in their efforts to know God and the supernatural. The mind is a vast area to explore, and there is much we do not know about it or about the possibility of extra-sensory perception. But let us be aware that God's word very strongly condemns placing faith in astrology, witchcraft, soothsaying and such like. Faith is to be placed in God alone, and He has revealed "all things pertaining to life and godliness," as we pointed out earlier in this lesson.

5. A valuable means of knowing God, one which is available to *everyone,* is that of spending QUIET TIMES WITH GOD. The psalmist advises: "Be still and know that I am God" (Psalms 46:10); and "Lie quietly upon your bed in silent meditation" (Psalms 4:4 Living Bible).

To be idle sometimes is a part of wisdom. It is the needful rest and relaxation which Christ invited his disciples to share with him when they were overstrained and worn out with labor. The best way to enjoy it is to get away from the crowd into some quiet place where the heart can be still with God. To lie quietly on one's bed in meditation is a good antidote for restlessness, for such times spent in communing with God and in digesting a recent Bible reading or study can be food for the soul and rest for the weary.

Too often we become so engrossed in our own busy little world that we no longer take the time to walk beside the still waters and to lie down in green pastures in meditation. Mrs. Lois Snead, writing in Christian Woman magazine, relates the following incident:

"One evening at dusk I looked out my kitchen window to see our three-year-old daughter lying on her back in the soft grass gazing contentedly at the sky. Quietly I went to her, "What are you doing, honey?" Serenely and confidently she replied, "Talking to God."

"Such unity with God is not easy to reach after childhood. It is hard for us to shed the cloak of self-indulgence and self-interest and come to God openly. The admonition to 'pray without ceasing' (1 Thessalonians 5:17) is a big order when the children are fighting, the television blaring, and the washing machine won't work. But prayer is our way over these frustrations. When prayer becomes our way of thought, when we have trained ourselves to pray about everything we are thinking or doing, we are rising to heights in knowing and loving God.

"Why not have certain prayers we say regularly as we perform daily routines? With a sink stacked with dirty dishes and a bin full of dirty clothes, why not thank God we are physically able to keep our house? As our toddlers leave a room strewn with toys or inventive play, why not thank God for their good minds? As we look into the eyes of a small boy whose mother and father give him no religious training, can we be thankful we have a little time and the opportunity to teach him of Jesus' love?"[5]

Our communion with God is not just the little snatches of time here and there that we can grasp amid our "busyness." To walk with God means to think of Him often, everywhere, and in every situation, to be constantly aware of His nearness. Then these few quiet times that we can find to be with Him alone we can treasure as precious moments with our dearest friend, for He is then no stranger to us. In addition to Bible study and prayer, we can use these times to practice the presence of God, impressing deeply upon the heart His divine existence. Try emptying your heart of all other things, letting God possess it alone. If we are with Him often—in quiet times, in busy times, in pleasure times—how can we be with Him thus, and not know Him?

6. By coming to know Him, I learn to LOVE Him more. Knowledge is commonly the measure of love—the more extensive our knowledge of God, the greater will be our love. I dare say that those among your friends and acquaintances that you love the most are those that you know the best. People are sometimes worried because they are told to love God and they cannot find such feelings within themselves. What are they to do? It is very difficult to sit and try to manufacture feelings. It is easier to ask myself, "If I were sure that I loved God, what would I do?" then find the answer, and go and do it. Often conduct conditions belief more than belief conditions conduct. Jesus said, "If you love me, you will keep my commandments." Is it not also true that in keeping his

commandments you will come to love Him more and know Him better?

It is only those who are willing to dare to follow Jesus who come to spiritual certainty. Knowing God so well—His motives, His complete good will—knowing Him for a long enough time to be sure of these things, to be certain that no pressures will make Him change—this is the kind of knowledge that builds trust in God which enables us to step out, like Enoch, and walk with God.

"In a celebrated passage, Arthur Gossip tells how he noticed in the Hebrides that you never get away from the sea. Inland it thrusts arms at you, at every turn you see its grayness or glitter; the tang and the roaring of its breakers come to nostril and ear. The ocean has soaked into the people's very soul, so that even in their music one can hear the sobbing and the cluck and the gurgling ripple of great waters.

"CHRISTIAN, THE COMMON DAY CAN SO BE PERMEATED WITH THE SCENTS AND SOUNDS AND MYSTERIES OF A GOD WHO WALKS BESIDE US. DESTINATION, ETERNITY— AT A WALK."[6]

FOR MEDITATION AND DISCUSSION:

How can I pray to God, and not be with Him?

How can I be with Him often, and not know Him?

How can I know Him, and not love Him?

How can I love Him, and not obey Him?

How can I obey Him unless He is real to me?

How can He be real to me if self—not He—is still at the center of my being?

FOOTNOTES:

1. Clovis Chappell, *Living Zestfully* (Nashville: Abingdon-Cokesbury Press, 1959), pp. 118-119.
2. Clovis Chappell, *Questions Jesus Asked* (Nashville: Abingdon Press, renewal 1976), pp. 176-177.
3. Ann Smithson, "Looking About," *Christian Woman,* February 1965, pp. 8-9.
4. Smithson, p. 9.
5. Lois Snead, "Looking Up For God," *Christian Woman,* February 1965.
6. Frederick B. Speakman, *The Salty Tang* (Old Tappan, NJ: Fleming H. Revell Co., 1954), pp. 124-125.

LESSON 5:
Peace of the Presence of Jesus
by Sandy Sibley

"Why are you afraid? Have you not faith?" Mark 4:40

LESSON SCRIPTURE: Mark 4:35-41
OTHER SCRIPTURES: John 14:1-27   Philippians 4:6-8
John 16:33   Matthew 6:25-34
Colossians 1:19-23 1 Thessalonians 5:23-24

In the Middle East soldiers stand poised, guns aimed, ready at any moment to break the silence with the stench of war. In Ireland both Protestants and Catholics engage in a civil war that ultimately causes the innocent to suffer most. The war is waged in the name of God. In Bangladesh the conflict takes the form of hunger, as a father searches futilely for enough food to keep his family alive one more day. A mother, suffering from starvation herself, tries unsuccessfully to nurse her baby. In Phnom Pen, people flee the city in panic as communist gorillas turn homes and businesses into ruin. The very old, the very young, and those too sick to leave await their fate helplessly. In Vietnam the cries of hundreds of war orphans can barely be heard, for no one is listening. In America this conflict best finds expression in needle marks up and down the arms of our youth who will resort to whatever means necessary to sustain their habits. In our country this year we will lose thousands of our youth because of drug overdose, and many thousands more will take their lives intentionally. Mothers and fathers will hold children for the last time today. Husbands and wives will be torn apart from the effects of war, and the families that do manage to stay together today will be filled with anxiety about tomorrow.

In such a world as this I am to talk to you about the peace of the presence of Jesus. Words cannot begin to communicate to you the inadequacy I feel. As I thought about this world we live in there are some questions that kept tormenting me. Is there any peace for our

45

world today? Surely there's never been a time in history filled with more unrest or confusion. Or has there?

What is peace anyway?

Perhaps we would do well to name some things that peace is not.

Peace	*Conflict*
Trust	Worry
Confidence	Fear
Joy	Anxiety

Now that we've thought a little about peace, what is the peace of the presence of Jesus?

Jesus, very near to his death, gathered to him those twelve men, whom he loved so very much. He knew their hearts were troubled; he knew they were anxious about the future. He knew that soon they must face, just as he must, suffering, persecution, physical and mental anguish and rejection such as men had never known before. Knowing all of these things, Jesus speaks to them, leaving them a legacy so rich that all the wealth of Solomon could not touch it. And it is our heritage today, as he has left recorded for us words for a troubled world.

"Let not your hearts be troubled . . ." (John 14:1-27).

"I have told you these things, so that in me you may have peace. In this world you will have trouble. But take heart! I have overcome the world." (John 16:33 NIV).

How is the peace Jesus gives us different from what the world has to offer?

1. The peace the world offers is based on external conditions. If the external conditions are not just right, peace is not possible.

2. The peace the world gives does not last.

3. The peace the world gives is not available to everyone, rather only to a given few who are in the right place at the right time.

The peace that Jesus gives:

1. Is not dependent on outward circumstances but rather is internal. Jesus promises us peace in the midst of a life that is plagued with difficulties.

2. Is everlasting—not temporary—and no one can take it from us.

3. Is available to anyone who is willing to crown him Lord of their life. In the life that has the peace of the presence of Jesus, there are several noticable things *missing* from their life as well as some wonderful qualities added.

There is the *ABSENCE OF INTERNAL CONFLICT*.

We are at peace *with God* through our relationship with Jesus (Ephesians 2:11-18).

Though the early Christians were experiencing great persecution and hardships, they were always writing and talking about the peace that was theirs because of the presence of Christ in their lives.

The greatest struggle and turmoil there is, is the conflict that exists when man is separated from God.

"For God was pleased to have all his fullness dwell in him, and through him to reconcile to himself all things, whether things on earth or things in heaven, by making peace through his blood, shed on the cross" (Colossians 1:19-20 NIV).

This absence of conflict also finds expression in our relationships with each other. I know that I would not have much of an understanding at all about Christ's peace if I did not see it in the lives of fellow Christians. And so many times when worries and cares would engulf me, the peace in thier lives would spill over into mine, and because of the Christ in them—the victory is mine. We have a responsibility to live at peace with one another (Ephesians 4:1-3).

The peace Jesus gives is one that exhibits itself in the *ABSENCE OF WORRY AND ANXIETY.*

This is an area in which we can really be of some help to each other! When I'm worried about something, please don't console me with "Oh, well, that's only natural" or "That's okay, that's just the mother in you." I don't want to be natural, I want to live above that! I don't want the mother in me to overcome the Christ in me. Please remind me that I have a Father who loves me and is caring for me and that all I need do is to trust Him.

"Have no anxiety about anything, but in everything by prayer and supplication with thanksgiving let your requests be made known to God. And the peace of God, which passes all understanding, will keep your hearts and your minds in Christ Jesus" (Philippians 4:6-7).

When someone we love is very sick and the doctor comes to explain their condition to us with long medical terms that we don't even begin to understand, we realize that we are not capable of making intelligent medical decisions concerning their welfare; so we put our whole confidence in that doctor, believing that he will do the best possible thing. We allow him complete freedom to treat or operate because we *trust* him.

If we can exhibit that much faith in the human who every day makes mistakes, why can't we place that same amount of trust in the one who loved us so much that He gave His own life for us? I've never really understood why it is that we can trust God with eternity—but we don't trust Him to handle today.

We have some specific instructions about things we can have complete peace about, because He promised to take care of these areas.

We are to have *freedom* from *worry* about the *necessities of this life!*

"Therefore I tell you, do not worry about your life, what you will eat or drink; or about your body, what you will wear. Is not life more important than food, and the body more important than clothes? Look at the birds of the air; they do not sow or reap or store away in barns, and yet your heavenly Father feeds them. Are you not much more valuable than they?" (Matthew 6:25-26 NIV).

When anxiety and preoccupation about the things of this world take root in lives *peace* cannot reign.

What is security to the Christian anyway? Until we can know that security for us is to be in the hands of God—whatever his will for us might be—then we will continue to be plagued with worries.

"The world says, 'Success is how much money you accumulate, how big your house is, how new your car, how fashionable your clothing.' Are these our measure of success and security? Are these our standards? If so, then by our standards Christ was an utter failure and Paul the most insecure person who ever lived. Do we believe that? We say we don't, but unless we have the confidence that God does know best and that Romans 8:28 means what it really says, then, our standards are very little better than the world's!

"To the Christian *security* is . . . .

1. Freedom from guilt of sins—and money can't buy that!
2. Godly help in meeting each day as it comes—and money can't buy that!
3. Confidence that we can overcome evil—and money can't buy that!
4. Power of the Spirit within us to accomplish all things in His name—and money can't buy that!
5. Mansion in heaven in the presence of God for all eternity—and money can't buy that!

"We have no reason to worry over food, clothing, housing and the things we want money to buy. Our Father, who made all this to start with, who keeps the universe in order—this same Father has told us he'll see we are provided for. And the condition on our part? Merely seek first his kingdom. In other words, put God and his will first in our hearts: then we know we'll have food to eat, clothes to wear and a place to live."[1]

There are other things we need never worry about—trouble, hardship, persecution, famine, nakedness, danger, sword, death, life, supernatural power, the present, the future, or even where we are (Romans 8:35-39).

Worry is something we learn. If we are a worrier now, it is because we've practiced it through the years. There are three practical ways we can stop. We need to (1) re-direct our thinking, Philippians 4:8; (2) we need to pray about everything; (3) we need to live one day at a time and find peace in our present situation. "Do not worry about tomorrow, for tomorrow will worry about itself. Each day has enough trouble of its own" (Matthew 6:34 NIV).

"Finally, brothers, whatever is true, whatever is noble, whatever is right, whatever is pure, whatever is lovely, whatever is admirable—if anything is excellent or praiseworthy—think about such things" (Philippians 4:8 NIV).

Unless we can have peace today where we are, we have nothing the world will want.

I am convinced that one reason we do not have more influence as Christians is not because we do not know the truth and how to communicate it in word, but because we have not yet learned to communicate it with our lives. I'm not saying members of the church are not benevolent, kind, honest, gentle and concerned with others. I think we are. But we can still be all of these things and not have the quality of life which proves our confidence in God beyond a shadow of doubt to anyone beholding our daily lives.

Benevolence, kindness, honesty, gentleness—all are godly charac-teristics, but even those in the world can develop these. What this lesson is about concerns the life which God's children alone are privileged to live—that life free from all the anxieties this old world can throw at us. Until we present to the world a life free from these, then we cannot have the total effect on them which God intends us to have. If our lives are no better than their own, all we are offering amounts to little more than a religion. And Christianity is certainly not that! It is necessary for us to understand that we hinder the gospel if our lives are bound up in worry, doubt or fear.

No matter what happens to be our present situation there are things about it we would change if we could. There are people who are easily dissatisfied with their situation—no matter what it is. *Philippians 4:11-13* is the picture of a happy man who is at peace. "For I have learned to be content whatever the circumstances. I know what it is to be in need, and I know what it is to have plenty. I have learned the secret of being content in any and every situation, whether well-fed or hungry, whether living in plenty or in want. I can do everything through him who gives me strength."

We need to learn to be happy where we are. Our children and our husbands will be influenced by it. The tone of our home will be determined by our attitude. The tone of our home will have more influence on how our children feel about Christianity in our lives than any words we could ever speak. Someday our situation may be more ideal than it is right now—but today we need God's peace right where we are. He wants us to have it. He wants the world to see it in our lives.

Bob Hendron made a statement at a seminar in New Orleans that made a lasting impression on me. He said, "The final hour is ours—why worry about the next minute? We may not know what is coming but we know *who* is coming!''

The life lived in the peace of the presence of Jesus is a life that is rid of fear. In the place of fear is a deep trust, a confidence, a relationship and a joy because Jesus is Lord!

In Mark 4:35-41, Jesus was awakened by his disciples because they were afraid of the storm. Even though Jesus was present with them, fear robbed them of their peace. Jesus described this as a lack of faith—a lack of confidence in Him. "Why are you afraid? Have you no faith?"

Hear the words of Jesus again in John 14, "Let not your hearts be troubled"—*TRUST*.

He went on to describe this trust as a trust that crowned him, Lord, master of a life.

This commitment exhibits itself with a great peace that is so evident when *trouble* does come. Job exhibited a great confidence in God when outward circumstances would have led him to believe God had forsaken him. The same confidence can be ours when we crown him Lord. And the natural fruit of his reign is a peace and a joy unspeakable! It has been said that "Joy is the flag you fly when the Prince of Peace is in residence within your heart."

"Say it in times of joy, 'Jesus Christ is Lord!' Lest we be sidetracked with lesser joys, preoccupied with lesser gladness, caught up more with the blessing than the Blesser, acknowledge Him as Lord.

"Say it in times of sadness, 'Jesus is Lord!' These times are but for a moment. Joy comes in the morning. Trouble is temporary. He is Lord forever. Let it ring in times of distress, 'Jesus is Lord!'

"Say it in times of bereavement, 'Jesus is Lord!' When death's shadow has stolen over our homes, is there any more glorious a fact? A loved one is gone—a chair is vacant. A heart is longing and crushed but Jesus is Lord!

"Say it in times of pressure, 'Jesus is Lord!' Who is He? He is the Lord! Where is He? Indwelling His own! Is there any pressure outside that is greater than He is inside? NO! 'Greater is he that is in you' (1 John 4:4).

"Say it in times of success, 'Jesus is Lord!' As human applause deafens you, as men would lift you up to heaven and crown you Lord, refuse it and hand the crown to Him. Beware, the Lord our God is one God. His glory He will not give to another. Jesus is Lord!

"Say it in times of decision, 'Jesus is Lord!' This is not your decision because your life is not yours. It is His alone! He is the way; walk in Him. He is the truth; believe Him. He is the life; let him live that life in your body. His decision is already made. You owe Him your blind and complete obedience. He is Lord of that decision.

"Say it in times of loneliness, 'Jesus is Lord!' Is the family gone and have friends forsaken you? You may be lonely but you are not alone. 'My Lord is near me all the time.' 'He will never leave me or forsake me.' 'If He is for us, who can be against us?'

"Say it in times of confusion, 'Jesus is Lord!' You have lost your way. You no longer have any idea what is more important and what is not. You don't understand any more. You cannot feel anything. You are bothered, baffled and bewildered. Shout it, 'Jesus is Lord!'

"Say it in times of crushing guilt, 'Jesus is Lord!' Is your head bowed down low in sorrow and despair? You are self-discovered, self-dejected, and self-disgusted. You have fallen and failed again. Hear the words and say them again, 'Jesus is Lord!'

"Say it in times of accusation, 'Jesus is Lord!' He is the Lord, Wonderful Counsellor. He understands. That is all that matters. Let the devil rage and roar like a lion. Let him accuse and deceive the world. But the Savior is King of Glory who tramples the young lion under His feet. He is the same . . . . yesterday, today, and forever.

"Say it in times of overwhelming challenge, 'Jesus is Lord!' Is the task too great? Is the sum too high? Is the strength demanded too much? Is there no logical way it can be done? Is the risk too risky, the challenge too challenging? If it were not that the Lord was on our side, we would have fought in vain. 'Be ye steadfast, unmovable, always abounding in the work of the Lord, forasmuch as ye know that your labour is not in vain in the Lord' (1 Corinthians 15:58).

"Say it in times of family trouble, 'Jesus is Lord!' Disharmony reigns. Misunderstanding prevails. Tempers flare. Communication is lost. Stalemates deadlock. Gloom settles. Positions are taken and battle lines are drawn. Hope fades. Panic threatens. Listen! Jesus is Lord! 'Where Jesus is there is Peace' (2 Corinthians 3:17). 'For He is Himself our peace.' "[2]

Jesus comes to give us peace and the only way to have his peace is in our willingness to yield our lives with our assets and liabilities, our joys and sorrows, our cares and anxieties in exchange for a new life—one that crowns him Lord. A life not steeped with worry and concern for its own needs, but one lost in its love for others.

It is a love that cares so much it overcomes fear and timidity and is able to share with a lost world that there is

ONE WAY—TO PEACE—THROUGH THE POWER—OF THE CROSS.

"May God himself, the God of peace, sanctify you through and through. May your whole spirit, soul and body be kept blameless at the coming of our Lord Jesus Christ. The one who calls you is faithful and he will do it" (1 Thessalonians 5:23, 24).

FOR FURTHER STUDY AND DISCUSSION:

1. Do our children learn fear from us? How? Do they see us draw strength from the Lord to overcome difficulties? How?

2. What is the antidote for fear? Study 1 John 4:18 and 2 Timothy 1:7-8.

3. Discuss the concept of the presence of Jesus as presented in the following: The life of Christ has been perpetuated on earth in the form of his body, the church. When one is baptized into Christ, the Lord adds him to the church (Acts 2:41, 47). He therefore becomes a member of the church, a member of the body of Christ (Galatians 3:28; 1 Corinthians 12:13). To be in Christ therefore means to be in the church. Since the ascension, Christ's place on earth has been taken by his body, the church. The church, then, is truly the presence of Christ.

What does this say to you as to:
    —the importance of the church?
    —your oneness with fellow Christians?
    —your ability to draw strength from one another?
    —the image you convey to those in the world?

FOOTNOTES:

1. Marge Green, Harding Lectureship, November 1975.
2. Jack R. Taylor, *The Key to Triumphant Living* (Nashville: Broadman Press, 1971), pp. 70-71. Used by permission.

LESSON 6:
Material Things

"Why do you discuss the fact that you have no bread?" Mark 8:17

LESSON SCRIPTURE: Mark 8:14-17   Matthew 16:5-12
OTHER SCRIPTURES: Matthew 19:16-30   1 Timothy 6:5-11
                   Mark 10:23   Ephesians 4:28
                   Luke 12:22-34   Isaiah 55:1-3

What a difference in mind-set of the disciples and of Jesus! In this passage of Mark 8 we find them together, in the same boat, headed for the same shore, having shared the same experiences of the day, but *miles apart* in thinking. Jesus "sighed deeply in his spirit" as he thought of the mistaken and corrupt minds of the Pharisees in seeking from him a sign from heaven verifying his claim to Messiahship—the disciples were preoccupied with the fact that they had forgotten to bring bread. The incredible thing is that the disciples were thinking of bread, the Pharisees of a sign, in spite of the fact that Jesus has just fed the 5,000, supplying both bread and a miraculous sign.

"Do you still not understand?" It seems to us that Jesus is certainly justified in asking such a question. "Don't you remember the five loaves for the five thousand, and how many baskets you gathered? Or the seven loaves for the four thousand, and how many basketfuls you gathered? How is it you don't understand that I was not talking to you about bread?" It is as if he is saying, "Why all the worry about bread? Don't you remember what happened, and haven't these experiences taught you that you need not worry about such things if you are with me?"

The fact is that God knows that man cannot live without bread just as surely as he knows that man cannot live by bread alone. Bread is God's gift and we are taught to pray, "Give us this day our daily bread." A keen interest in bread, in satisfying hunger, runs through the entire ministry of Jesus. Surely our Lord demonstrates that he is interested in the whole man.

"He is therefore as truly interested in the bread that gives life to the body as he is in the bread that gives life to the soul. Our failure to realize this has led to a conviction regarding Jesus that has resulted in untold harm. That conviction is that Jesus is not quite practical. His teachings are, of course, unspeakably beautiful. He is indeed the 'sweet Galilean dreamer.' If we only lived in castles in the air, or if we were souls without any bodies, then his teachings might be excellent. But since we have bodies that must be housed and clothed and fed, we had better look elsewhere for teaching that fits us to live the life that now is.

"But this view is flatly contradictory to the teaching of Jesus. Our Lord is interested in *all* our interests. He never drew any sharp distinction between the secular and the sacred as we are accustomed to do. With Jesus, religion permeated the whole of life. He knew that for one to be religious on holy days and in holy places was not in reality to be religious at all. Jesus, therefore, was interested in the temporal as well as the spiritual."[1]

And yet we see him, it would seem, a little "put out" with the disciples over the direction of their thinking. Why? The answer is obvious. Hunger was not the danger threatening them at this time. Jesus was issuing a valid warning against a very real danger. "Be on your guard against the leaven of the Pharisees and Sadducees." Remember that, to the Jew, "leaven" meant corruption or evil. What did Jesus mean when he warned against the evil influence of the Pharisees and Sadducees?

Since the Pharisees saw religion in terms of laws and commandments and rules and regulations, this is a warning against a religion of externalism. To put it in modern terms, it is a warning against a religion of outward respectability, which looks on a man's outward actions and forgets the inner state of the heart. Since the Sadducees were wealthy and aristocratic, Jesus may have been warning them against giving material things too high a place in their scheme of values.

Jesus was urging the disciples to turn their minds from the materialistic to more important and more lasting considerations. Rather than giving all their attention to material bread, he would have them remember that "the bread of God is that which comes down from heaven, and gives life to the world . . . I am the bread of life; he who comes to me shall not hunger, and he who believes in me shall never thirst" (John 6:33-35).

Are we, like the disciples, guilty of materialism? In a nation of plenty, with a large percentage of the population overweight, and diet books listed among the best sellers, perhaps our attention needs to be turned from material bread to spiritual bread. Then, we can

"delight in fatness," according to the wisdom of Isaiah:
  "Why do you spend your money for that which is not bread,
    and your labor for that which does not satisfy?
  Hearken diligently to me, and eat what is good,
    and delight yourselves in fatness" (Isaiah 55:2).
Probably, we would all agree that spiritual bread is more valuable than the material; but the problem, as always, is translating this value into everyday living in a materialistic world. Let us honestly examine our thinking and our actions on this very vital subject.

Materialism
by Shirlee Lawson

Are we, today, guilty of the same materialistic outlook as were the disciples, who had just witnessed the miraculous feeding of the multitude? Is such a materialistic viewpoint evident in discussions on television, and in our own discussions with neighbors and friends? Do we follow the admonition in Luke 12:22, "Therefore I tell you, do not be anxious about your life, what you shall eat, nor about your body, what you shall put on"?

In discussing materialism, we need to establish what materialism is. A simple definition is "the tendency to care too much for the things of this world and neglect spiritual needs." Are any of us guilty of this? In what ways?

IDOLATRY is defined as the paying of honor to any CREATED object. We are not very sympathetic with Old Testament idol worship, but what do you suppose the people of that time would think if they were projected into our world today? Just based on their observations, do you think they might feel that some of us worship our homes, cars, family, cleanliness, health, bodies, appearance, pleasure, public image?

I think this is a lesson we all need, but I have found it a very difficult one to teach. After much soul searching, I concluded that, as in all spiritual matters—and this is a spiritual matter—the New Testament is our only valid source of information as to the proper attitude toward this dilemma. In the first place, my own opinion changed somewhere along the line. Smugly, I thought I had it all figured out, what with all my reading, research, etc.

We say everything we have belongs to the Lord. I'm afraid this is an element or dimension of New Testament Christianity that we have missed out on, for the most part. Is it easy to be sincere about our faith when our faith doesn't make much difference, anyway?

COVETOUSNESS brings up another point. We all agree that covetousness is sin. But doesn't materialism breed covetousness? We are bombarded on all sides by the advertizing media, as well as peer pressure, with such statements as YOU NEED, YOU DESERVE,

YOU OWE IT TO YOURSELF, YOU'VE COME A LONG WAY BABY, GRAB ALL THE GUSTO YOU CAN GET. We are programmed to WANT, WANT, WANT. Then we begin to spend a lot of time and energy to get what we want.

Materialism breeds selfishness, also. Francis Schaeffer makes the statement that all sin springs from selfishness. Think about that for a minute and then try to name a sin that does not have selfishness at its base. Materialism focuses attention on ME and MINE, always looking inward. It robs us of our interest in others and their needs. Every person has just so much time and just so much capacity. If this is all, or most all, consumed by home, my family, my appearance, my needs and desires, there can't be much left.

Most of us live in our "Ivory Tower," pretty well insulated from the suffering of the world, but the New Testament principle is "TO WHOM MUCH IS GIVEN, MUCH IS EXPECTED." So then, since we live in the United States, can we have a detached attitude toward the rest of the world? What about the suffering right here in our own country?

But understand this, that in the last days there will come times of stress. For men will be lovers of self, lovers of money, proud, arrogant, abusive, disobedient to their parents, ungrateful, unholy, inhuman, implacable, slanderers, profligates, fierce, haters of good, treacherous, reckless, swollen with conceit, lovers of pleasure rather than lovers of God, holding the form of religion but denying the power of it. Avoid such people.

For among them are those who make their way into households and capture weak women, burdened with sins and swayed by various impulses, who will listen to anybody and can never arrive at a knowledge of the truth (2 Timothy 3:1-7).

Do these words describe us?

Now, after having said all of that, we are getting to the meat of the coconut, and this is where we really must rely on the New Testament.

HOW MUCH IS TOO MUCH?

I wish I could tell you. We are all looking for a magic formula— 10%, 15%, 20%, 50%—but doesn't it really depend on what is left after the gift is given and on our attitude?

In Mark 12:41, we read that the rich cast in MUCH. Some say that the Jews gave as much as 40% before they were through tithing, even down to the smallest herbs and spices. Jesus said that the rich just cast into the treasury out of their ABUNDANCE, and they were not commended for it, even though it was a very large amount. Here it might be well for us to settle the question of whether we belong to the rich or poor of the world. To which class do you think you belong? Why?

We all rationalize about the things we have, the things we want, and the things we spend our money for.

A may have a nicer house than B.

B may spend more on furniture than C, who spends a lot on clothes.

D may buy a new boat instead of a new car.

E may take a long vacation instead of doing any of the other things. Most of us spend our money as we please, according to our individual tastes and income.

NEW TESTAMENT CHRISTIANS HAD A DIFFERENT VIEW OF LIFE. We read over and over again of their sharing with one another and with those in need. Do you think we would be that generous? Or would we just give of our abundance. Consider carefully the following Scriptures:

Romans 12:1-2. Are we transformed or conformed?

1 John 2:15. Love not the world.

Luke 12:34. Where our treasure is, our heart will be.

1 Thessalonians 4:11-12. Tells us what our ambition for life should be.

1 Timothy 6:6-10. Teaches godliness and contentment.

BEING A DISCIPLE OF CHRIST IS COSTLY. Matthew 16:24 tells us to deny self and take up the cross. That, I'm sure, means different things to each of us, but it is something to which we all ought to give serious thought.

This discussion may have raised more questions than it has answered. What I hoped to accomplish was to motivate all of us to examine our own hearts and lives in the light of the teaching and examples which we find in the New Testament. May I leave you this final thought:

For you know the grace of our Lord Jesus Christ, that though He was RICH, yet for your sakes He became POOR, so that by His poverty you might be RICH (2 Corinthians 8:9). Rich indeed!

FOR FURTHER STUDY AND DISCUSSION:

1. Discuss how materialism compares with idolatry. Ask yourself, "to what am I really devoted?"

2. If material things are given by God to be *used,* rather than collected, (see Ephesians 4:28) where do we draw the line between legitimate use and unlawful accumulation?

3. Which of the following may be obstacles to *your* using and sharing material possessions?

    a. Luxurious living.

    b. Fear of insecurity.

    c. Pride or respectability.

Can you name others?

BOOKS: Linsell, Harold *The World, the Flesh and the Devil*
Larson, Bruce *Living on the Growing Edge*
Smith, Charles Merrill *The Case of the Middle Class Christian*

FOOTNOTES:

1. Clovis Chappell, *Questions Jesus Asked* (Nashville: Abingdon Press, renewal 1976), p. 63.

LESSON 7:
Treasures New and Old
by Carol Barnett Robertson

"Have you understood all this? . . . Every Scribe who has been trained for the kingdom of heaven is like a householder who brings out of his treasure what is new and what is old." Matthew 13:51-52

LESSON SCRIPTURE: Matthew 13:34-52   Ephesians 2:14
OTHER SCRIPTURES: 2 Corinthians 4:16-18   Matthew 5:17
                               Malachi 3:6   2 Corinthians 5:17
                               1 Corinthians 15:51-52   1 Corinthians 13

Revelation 21:5
1 John 3:2
1 Peter 4:10
Ephesians 4:23-24
Genesis 1:1
Revelation 21:1

OUTLINE

Treasures New and Old

Introduction: Change
   I   Old and New Worship
   II   Old and New Self
   III Old and New Heaven
Conclusion

Jesus teaches a parable in which he likens the scribe who has been made a disciple to the kingdom of heaven, to the householder who brings forth from his treasures, things new and old (Matthew 13:51-53).

59

Life is full of beginnings and endings with *change* the process in the interim.

"Change, the father of progress, is at the same time the mother of anxiety." In his article "To Change or Not to Change," Mission Magazine, August 1970, Arthur L. Miley discusses 'Change' and I have freely adapted some of his thoughts.

While change is a constant force in life, man has always had a tendency to fight it. His resistance stems from FEAR; change threatens the stability of the known (old), which is safe and comfortable, and opens up all the uncertainties and anxieties of the unknown (new).

Today we are living in a period in which the scope and rapidity of change are greater than they have ever been before. Our habits, traditions and values are constantly challenged; our minds are continually bombarded by new concepts, techniques and re-orientations.

Life is a continuous process and whether we will it or not, change is inevitable. Change can be positive or regressive, or it can be an ungoverned drift.

Will Durant said, "Every custom begins as a broken precedent." We have three choices:

1. Managing change positively.
2. Accepting change positively.
3. Becoming the victim of change.

Paul said, "Prove all things; hold fast that which is good" (1 Thessalonians 5:21 KJV).

There are in our own church many instances of change in our order of worship, in method of giving, in our literature and sermon topics, and, most recently, our attitudes toward and teaching of the Holy Spirit.

Where change is not allowed, such as in the Shaker or Amish groups, the religion becomes stagnant and may die. In our own lifetime we've seen the Catholic Church struggle to change and become more relevant to the individual member.

Without change, maturity is impossible. How sad to see children who don't grow up, both physically and mentally. How tragic to see adults who refuse to accept responsibilities, and try to remain forever teenagers. How hopeless to see Christians who are unable to progress from receivers to givers, from learners to teachers of the Word.

Make every change a new milepost toward our best possible selves.

1. We know that we reap what we sow.
2. "And the world passes away and the lust of it; but he who does the will of God abides forever" (1 John 2:17).

It should readily be recognized that there is a progression of knowledge. We build today on that which was discovered yesterday.[1]

OLD AND NEW WORSHIP

"I the Lord do not change" (Malachi 3:6). Of what value is the study of the Old Testament today?

"Have you understood all this?" He asked; and they answered, "Yes." He said to them, "When, therefore, a teacher of the law has become a learner in the kingdom of Heaven, he is like a householder who can produce from his store both the new and the old" (Matthew 13:51, 52).

"The allusion is to the fact that a good householder, in entertaining his guests, brings forth from his treasure of provisions, both articles long laid away for special occasions, and new ones recently provided. So the Christian scribe or teacher brings forth the instruction of his hearers both the old lessons with which he has long been familiar, and new ones he has but recently acquired. While teaching others, he is himself a learner, and he is able, out of the new or the old, to find something suitable to every class of hearers."[2]

"The disciples were to be themselves teachers, bring out new truths from the store of what they had learned from the Master . . . and at the same time revealing the *inner beauty and true meaning* of the Old Testament teaching."[3]

Once again: of what value is the study of the Old Testament to a Christian?

When Jesus said he came not to destroy the law, but to fulfill it (Matthew 5:17), what value was he placing on the Old Law?

The Authority of the Past

"It is, of course, always good to know what our ancestors accepted as truth. In many cases it is good to agree to accept what they have accepted. But it is always dangerous to suppose that we can believe what they believed without first weighing carefully their theories and determining whether the theories fit the facts derived from our experience. Jesus knew well the theories of his Jewish ancestors and had respect for them. In fact, much of what he taught seems to have its basis in the Old Testament. But he did not hesitate to question and reject much that he received from 'the Former Age.' 'Ye have heard that it hath been said, an eye for an eye, and a tooth for a tooth,' said Jesus, 'But I say unto you, that ye resist not evil: but whosoever shall smite thee on thy right cheek, turn to him the other also' (Matthew 5:38-39 KJV).

"We have too many religious people in our time who are more cautious than Jesus was. Such people, though they may have discovered some errors in what they call 'modernism,' have come to the conclusion that whatever is new or modern is necessarily

wrong. What is modern may be wrong, of course; but it should not
be considered wrong because it is modern. The tendency among
religious people to find something that seems to be spiritually
rewarding and then to stop and say that any change will ruin what
we have discovered or any attempt to improve what we have will
surely destroy it is a very dangerous one. If Calvin or Luther
(or Campbell) could improve what they received from their
ancestors, then their followers can also improve what they have
received from them. One need not suppose that he is improving the
Bible! He may, however, progress a great deal in his understanding
of it and in his application of it to his age.''[4]

"Gentiles and Jews, he has made the two one, and in his own
body of flesh and blood has broken down the enmity which stood
like a dividing wall between them; for he anulled the law with its
rules and regulations, so as to create out of the two a single new
humanity in himself, thereby making peace" (Ephesians 2:14 NEB).

"When anyone is united to Christ, there is a new world; the old
order has gone, and a new order has already begun" (2 Corinthians
5:17 NEB).

Jesus denounced the religion of his day, but did not renounce it!

Keith Miller in his book, *The Taste of New Wine* writes:
"Historians are amazed that a handful of virtually uneducated men
by the world's standards, with no social or political connections of
importance; no program—no systematic theology or plan—no
budget—no mass media (or even the corpus of the New Testament
for several hundred years)—could begin transforming a large part of
the whole world's concept of the character and purpose of God for
men. It is particularly baffling that this one sect burst forth from the
empty tomb and began covering the earth. Even acknowledging the
tremendously propitious time in history which Christ came, the
development of Christianity *is* amazing.''[5]

God sacrificed His Son, who left as His legacy His church. What
have we done with it? Let us briefly trace the history and changes in
the development of the Christian church.

The early church was spontaneous and free, its message was
urgent and Christians were excited. Later, the church became more
and more restricted as power and influence became centrally located
in Rome. When this power spread throughout the Western World, it
became almost a stranglehold on the religious *and* secular lines of
the people. Thus the Reformation burst forth and Martin Luther left
this legacy for us.

Martin Luther's Achievement

1. He began with the basic assumption that the Holy Scriptures
were the truth from the beginning to the end. His life was an

unending assault on those who assailed the authority of that word.

2. Martin Luther had absolute confidence in the validity of God's Word and brought the Bible and its teaching to the common people. He believed every man ought to know the Word of God from a personal knowledge and not merely second hand from a priest or pastor.[6]

Restoration of First Century Christianity

In the 19th Century the movement we call the Restoration Movement began the trend toward an ecumenical or non-denominational gathering of Christians. Thus we see how our worship of God has come full circle, back to a 1st Century idea of church as "spontaneous and free, with an urgent message and excited Christians."

To the Pharisees, anything different was irreverent.

How can we distinguish between what is truth for all ages and what is tradition?

In "Make Love your Aim," Eugenia Price says: "When God is limited by what happens to be the familiar to us, love in us is stopped dead in its tracks. When we grow so comfortable in the surroundings which happen to be familiar to us that God is trapped in either the jig-time tempo of a gospel chorus or the lofty strains of a Bach Chorale, we are missing *love*. And God is missing a chance to love through us."[7]

Again: How can we distinguish between what is truth for all ages and what is tradition? By *Love:*

A love for God's Word that leads to an honest and open search for truth rather than for proof of one's own opinions or preconceived ideas.

A love for people which desires salvation of souls above any selfish interest, pride or tradition.

A love for the opportunity to worship with fellow believers which reaches beyond the printed "order of worship" to joyful communion with God.

In the 13th chapter of 1 Corinthians we read that love knows no limit to its endurance, no end to its trust, no fading of its hope; it can outlast anything. It is, in fact, the one thing that still stands when all else is fallen.

OLD AND NEW SELF

"Behold, I make all things new" (Revelation 21:5).

"It does not yet appear what we shall be, but we know that when

He appears we shall be like Him, for we shall see Him as He is" (1 John 3:2).

From his article in "Mission" magazine, *Notes on Revolution,* Don Haynes writes, "The Christian salvation process is itself a revolution. The New Testament speaks of 'new men,' not changed men. Paul admonished the Roman Christians to 'be transformed,' not reformed. The terminology is significant. Creation of something new is implied, as opposed to modification of the old order of things. A 'new birth' is not an overhaul or an adjustment—or a change of denominational affiliation."[8]

William Barclay in his *Commentary on Matthew,* said that Jesus never desired or intended that any man should forget all he knew when he comes to Him; but he should use it in a new service.

"Every man comes to Jesus Christ with some gift and with some ability. Jesus does not ask that man should give up his gift. So many people think that when a man declares for Christ, he must give things up, and concentrate on what are so-called religious things. A business man need not give up his business; rather he should run it as a Christian would run it. One who can sing, or dance, or act, or paint need not give up his art, but must use his art as a Christian would use it. The sportsman need not give up his sport, but must play as a Christian would play. Jesus did not come to empty life but to fill it, not to impoverish life but to enrich it. Here we see Jesus telling men, not to abandon their gifts, but to use them even more wonderfully because they are using them in the light of the Knowledge which He has given them."[9]

Sin has been defined as "missing the mark." "Each one, as a good manager of God's different gifts, must use for the good of others the special gift he has received from God" (1 Peter 4:10 TEV).

"You must be made new in mind and spirit, and put on the new nature of God's creating, which shows itself in the just and devout life called for by the truth" (Ephesians 4:23, 24 NEB).

J. B. Phillips in "Your God is Too Small," writes: "The religion of Jesus Christ changes people (if they are willing to pay the price of being changed) so they quite naturally and normally live as 'sons and daughters of God,' and of course exert an excellent influence on the community."[10]

Keith Miller in his book, "A Second Touch" wrote: "I now began to see that all my past was training me for the events and encounters of *this day,* however insignificant the day may seem from my perspective . . . . I saw in the Scriptures that the days on which Christ was born, crucified and rose from the dead did *not* seem important *as they were happening* even to most of the people present, but only to those who saw the events of those days from God's perspective."

In C. S. Lewis' book "Beyond Personality," he speaks of the process of evolution, noting the past, and wondering what will be the Next Step for "the New Men."

"The Christian view is that The Next Step has already appeared, and it is really new—a change from being creatures of God to being Sons of God. The step from being creatures to sons is voluntary in the sense that we can accept or refuse it. One gets it, not by heredity, but by personal contact with Him."[12]

C. S. Lewis calls this the "good infection;" other men become new by being in Him and losing themselves!

Life is full of beginnings and endings with change the process in the interim. It is up to us to make every change a new milepost toward our best possible selves.

OLD AND NEW HEAVEN

"In the beginning God created the heavens and the earth. And God saw everything that He had made, and behold, it was very good" (Genesis 1:1, 31).

When beginning this study, I soon realized that the direction I *had* to take was toward our ultimate goal, heaven. When God created earth, He intended for it to be heaven. Yet, through the passage of time and the sinfulness of man, this "heaven" all too often becomes a hell on earth. If the old heaven was earth, the earth that God created for Adam and Eve, then the new heaven is the one spoken of by John in Revelation 21:1, "And I saw a new heaven and a new earth: for the first heaven and the first earth were passed away; and there was no more sea" (KJV).

Heaven is our goal; yet it is a goal that requires death. Death is a trauma for those who experience it and for those who witness it, for our family and friends. We must go *through* death to heaven. But over and over again we read of our talk with someone who has "died" or so nearly reached death, that he can actually relate the experience of death to us. Almost without exception we hear that, to them, death was a separation as simple as moving from one room to another, from one body to another, from one life to another. The fear is gone, the regrets are not there, and a future, a very real future, is opening up. Some even resent, momentarily, being brought back to life.

Marie Curie said, "Nothing in life is to be feared, it is only to be understood."

Also, we know that borrowing trouble from the future does not deplete the supply.

How can we learn to accomplish the miracle of going through death to heaven?

J. B. Phillips in "Your God is Too Small" writes, " 'Heaven' is not, so to speak, the reward for being a good boy, (tho many people seem to think so), but is the continuation and expansion of a quality of life which begins when a man's central confidence is transferred from himself to God-become-man. This 'faith' links him here and now with truth and love, and it is significant that Jesus Christ on more than one occasion is reported to have spoken of 'eternal life' as being entered into *now,* tho plainly to extend without limitation (forever and ever) after the present incident we call life. The man who believes in the authenticity of His message and puts his confidence in it already possesses the quality of 'eternal life.' "[13]

"He who believes in the Son has eternal life" (John 3:36). "Truly, truly, I say to you, he who hears my word and believes him who sent me, has eternal life" (John 5:24).

The same thought is expressed again in John 6:47.

If we accept this we shall not be too surprised to find Christ teaching an astonishing thing about physical death, not merely that it is an experience robbed of its terror, but that as an experience it *does not exist at all.* "If anyone keeps my word, he will never see death" (John 8:51). And "whoever lives and believes in me shall never die" (John 11:26).

It is impossible to avoid the conclusion that the meaning that Christ intended to convey was that death was a completely negligible experience to the man who has already begun to live life of the eternal quality.

"Jesus Christ hath abolished death" wrote Paul many years ago, but there have been very few since his day who appear to have believed it.

"Hold to God's Unchanging Hand"

Time is filled with Swift Transition
Naught of earth unmoved can stand,
Build your hopes on things eternal
Hold to God's Unchanging Hand.

Trust in Him who will not Leave you,
Whatsoever years may bring,
If by earthly friends forsaken
Still more closely to Him Cling.

When your journey is completed,
If to God you have been true
Fair and bright the home is glory
Your enraptured soul will view.

Build your hopes on things eternal
Hold to God's Unchanging hand.

"No wonder we do not lose heart! Though our outward humanity is in decay, yet day by day we are inwardly renewed. Our troubles are slight and short lived; and their outcome an eternal glory which outweighs them far. Meanwhile our eyes are fixed, not on the things that are seen, but on the things which are unseen: for what is seen passes away; what is unseen is eternal" (2 Corinthians 4:16-18 NEB).

QUESTIONS FOR DISCUSSION

1. How should we as Christians view change? In our homes, in our churches, in our world?
2. Of what value is the study of the Old Testament today, with references to change?
3. What value did Jesus place on the old law?
4. What have we done with the legacy of Christ, the church? Trace history and changes.
5. How can we distinguish between what is truth for all ages and what is tradition?
6. How should Christians change and how should they *not* change? Discuss talents, knowledge and growth.
7. Discuss the Christian view of death and the gift of "eternal life." When does heaven begin?

FOOTNOTES:

1. Arthur L. Miley, *Mission,* August 1970.
2. McGarvey, *Commentary on Matthew* (Delight, AR: Gospel Light Co.), p. 126.
3. New Bible Commentary (Grand Rapids, MI: Eerdman's Publishing Co.), p. 790.
4. "Job," The Living Word Adult Study (Austin, TX: Sweet Publications, 1965), pp. 24-25.
5. Keith Miller, *Taste of New Wine* (Waco, TX: Word Books, 1965), pp. 114-115. Used by permission of Word Books.
6. N. Tjernagel, *The Reformation Era* (St. Louis: Concordia Publishing House), p. 36.
7. Eugenia Price, *Make Love Your Aim* (Grand Rapids, MI: Zondervan Publishing House, 1967), p. 132.
8. Don Haynes, "Notes on Revolution," *Mission,* December 1970.
9. William Barclay, *The Gospel of Matthew, Vol. 2* (Philadelphia: Westminster Press), pp. 90-91.
10. J.B. Phillips, *Your God is Too Small* (New York: MacMillan Publishing Co., 1953), p. 132.
11. Keith Miller, *A Second Touch* (Waco, TX: Word Books, 1967), p. 61.
12. C.S. Lewis, "The New Man," *Beyond Personality* (New York: MacMillan Publishing Co.), pp. 182-183.
13. Phillips, p. 128.

LESSON 8:
Family Relationships

"Who is my mother, and who are my brothers?"
Matthew 12:48

LESSON SCRIPTURE: Matthew 12:46-50   Mark 3:31-35
OTHER SCRIPTURES: 1 John 3   Romans 12:9-10
                1 Corinthians 12:12-27   1 Peter 1:22
                                   Titus 2:3-5

Many of the questions which Jesus asked are thought-provoking and soul-searching, with no definitive solution apparent. But this question He answered Himself, in the next breath, and with a positive finality. "And stretching out his hand toward his disciples, he said, 'Here are my mother and my brothers! For whoever does the will of my Father in heaven is my brother, and sister, and mother.' "

Thus did Jesus sanction the relationships of a spiritual family, whose members spring from the same Father (Ephesians 3:14-15; 1 John 3:1), and who have been washed in the same cleansing blood (1 John 1:7). Paul gives further illumination to this concept as he speaks of the "household of faith" in Galations 6:10 and explains in Ephesians 2:19 that "you are fellow citizens with the saints and members of the household of God, built upon the foundation of the apostles and prophets, Christ Jesus himself being the cornerstone." In addition, the writer of Hebrews gives assurance that "we are (God's) house if we hold fast our confidence and pride in our hope."

The relationship of a human family is as old as "in the beginning" when God created Adam and Eve and told them to be fruitful and multiply. Since that time, the family has not ceased to be an important part of existence on this earth and a determining influence on the mores of the times. And I am convinced that, as an institution, it will weather the onslaught of the "new morality" and

69

the rising divorce rate. As these influences reek more and more havoc upon society, we may see a swing of the pendulum back to what some might call the old-fashion family, with its closeness and its roots bound into ideas originating in God's Word. There are many sociologists and criminologists, even among non-religious people, who agree that the return to family life is the only solution to the ills that beset our crime-ridden society.

Surely, of all people, we Christians, as God's people, should be doing all within our power to affect this return and to show by our example what a high value we place on the family. And yet we find that divorce is creeping rapidly into the church and delinquency among our teenagers is no longer a surprise. Why? Have we failed to prize the family as something very valuable? Have we let our "busyness" deprive us of one of the greatest blessings life has to offer?

"How many do you know who have been granted that most sacramental of all relationships, the human family, and have taken for granted its privileges, assuming it would always be there to enjoy; but while they were busy here and there, the years, so brimful of that blessing, have poured out their contents and are gone!"[1]

How many fathers have been too busy climbing the ladder of success in their profession, or even just "making a living," to be a real dad to their children? How many mothers have been so busy working to accumulate "things," or to provide their children with lessons for "this" and "that," that they have missed many precious childhood moments? Or how many mothers have been too busy keeping a perfect house or entertaining friends to take a walk in the woods or show enthusiasm over a frog or a turtle? How many parents have succumbed to such a crowded schedule that there was no time left to squeeze in family devotionals, family talk sessions or even very many family meals?

If we have been lax in taking advantage of the privileges of family life, we may have been even more so in regard to the spiritual family. And yet it is true that the possibilities of this spiritual kinship hold relationships of inestimable value. The ties that bind Christians together can be even stronger than those of flesh and blood.

"True kinship is not always a matter of flesh and blood relationship. Sometimes a man's nearest and dearest are the people who understand him least, and he finds his true fellowship with those who work for a common ideal and who share a common experience. People who are very different in their background, their mental equipment, and even their methods, can be firm friends if they have before them a common ideal, for which they work, and toward which they press.

"If kinship comes from a common goal, then Christians above all men possess its secret, for all of us are seeking to know Christ better and to bring others within His Kingdom. If kinship lies in a common experience, Christians have the common experience of being forgiven sinners, and the fellowship of laughing and weeping together."[3]

"If one member suffers, all suffer together; if one member is honored, all rejoice together. Now you are the body of Christ and individually members of it" (1 Corinthians 12:26-27).

Recently, I crushed my elbow in a fall. Immediately, my whole body was wracked with pain. Using Paul's analogy of the church as a body, I can easily understand that where true fellowship and family spirit exist, what one member experiences in suffering or joy affects all those who are bound in a bundle of life with him. The church is a sharing fellowship, a circle of love, a devoted family.

"Whoever does the will of my Father in heaven," said Jesus, "is my brother, and sister, and mother." The relationship of brothers and sisters in Christ is a precious privilege, with both rewards and heartaches. The following study of the subject of "Sisters" was made especially for this lesson by Mrs. C. P. Seabrook, a devoted Christian, Bible student and teacher, and one highly esteemed by her own sisters in Christ.

SISTERS IN CHRIST

Jesus taught in parables, using objects familiar to his disciples in order to teach a lesson. Some 50-odd of these parables are recorded—the mustard seed, the sower, the pearl of great price, the good shepherd and the lost sheep, for example. These things his hearers could understand. Likewise, God has given us the relationship in the church of brothers and sisters, a concept which He knew that we could understand. It behooves us to look into this relationship and learn the lesson of the attitudes He intends us to have toward our brothers and sisters in Christ.

The terms "brothers," "brethren," "fellowship," carry with them the idea of the whole body and a concept of sharing. Recently, I was privileged to hear a series of sermons on the subject of witnessing. The message of these lessons was that the early church witnessed in three ways: words, deeds and fellowship. As I listened, I was further impressed with the importance of witnessing of Christ through fellowship. Our relation, one with another, is a witness to the world.

There have been volumes written on the relationship of husband and wife, parent and child, but I have found nothing written about the relationship between sisters other than what is said in the Bible. Therefore, I find myself looking at the relationship of my physical sister and myself to discover both the negative and the positive qualities, and I will assure you there are some negative ones. But we shall try to see how we may translate some of the positive qualities into our lives in the spiritual body as sisters of Christ.

First, let us get rid of the negative aspects. I shall have to look back into my childhood because most of the negative qualities between my sister and myself were predominant back in our childhood days. Although I was three years younger than she, the reality of that fact never seemed to dawn on me. Everything that she had looked a little bit better than what I had, and I was forever wanting what she had rather than my own. I was very jealous of her being the first to get everything and of the things she was allowed to do. Even the way she wore her hair—with the little "spit-curls"—was a source of envy, as I had to wear the straight "Buster Brown." This was very irritating! When she put up her dolls and turned to more grown-up activities, I put mine up too; and I thought I should be allowed to do everything that she did. Of course, that brought rebellion on her part. Mother would say, "Oh, let her go with you," but my sister would reply, "I would as soon stay home, if she has to go!" Since that statement hurt my feelings, the whole incident brought on conflict. It was the envious, jealous attitude on my part which brought on much of the conflict between us. Of course, such an attitude is childish and immature; but, thankfully, I outgrew it.

I think we should look into this childish attitude of jealousy and envy in the church. If we, who are younger, have those negative qualities in our hearts, let us try to recognize them as childish and immature, to put them off and to mature. We who are older and still have these qualities—we should be ashamed!

As my sister and I matured, we became more tolerant, more understanding, and were able to overlook many of our differences. We are entirely different personalities, with different opinions; and, even as we grew older, we would have some very heated arguments. We had very opposite views on politics, but as we grew older we would overlook points of disagreement, and we developed a forgiving spirit.

Recently, as we were talking about our long life together, we realized that we have been privileged to be together frequently; for, even after we were married, we lived in the same town for a number of years. Our husbands were very compatible, and we had a very close relationship. Being together as much as we have, and being different personalities, and holding different opinions, we may have done and said things that would hurt one another. We tried to recall reasons for our hurt feelings or anger, but neither of us could think of a single one! Do you know what this is? It is *true forgiveness*! We could not bring up a single instance and give the reason for it! If we could be as forgiving with our sisters in Christ as we are our natural sisters, would it not be wonderful?

Do you know why we are truly forgiving of our sister? We make allowances; we give them the benefit of the doubt; we know they love us. I *know* that my sister loves me. I know that if she says something that rubs me the wrong way, she does not really mean to hurt me, and I know her motives are pure. If we could just feel the same way toward our sisters in Christ and say, "There is love in her heart; her motive is right," if we could just be that tolerant and understanding and forgiving of our sisters in Christ, would it not be wonderful? That is something that we have in our relationship as natural sisters that we should translate into our spiritual relationship.

Possibly the biblical character of Joseph is the epitome of forgiveness. You know, the answer to forgiving is not what men deserve—we must remember that. We may say, "She got her just deserts—she deserved it!" But this is not a forgiving attitude. I don't suppose anyone had any more heinous crimes committed against him than did Joseph; but when his brothers were in need, he opened his heart to them and met their every need. This is *true* forgiveness. He held no rancor, no grudge. To have that true forgiving spirit is something that we need among Christians.

Of course, the basis of all our relationships is love. There is a natural affection in the family. You have heard, no doubt, the expression that "blood is thicker than water"? The meaning of this old expression is that a person will rally to the cause of someone who is kin to them and will defend them, regardless of cost. We had this illustrated in a negative way by the Hatfields and McCoys in Kentucky. These families fueded and fought, generation after generation, just because they were blood-kin. We do have a loyalty in the blood relationship.

Paul, in speaking to Timothy, mentions a time, "the latter days," when there would be a lack of this natural affection; but this lack is abnormal, for there is a natural affection that we have by being blood-kin. In the spiritual family, let us let the blood of Christ be the bond that will unite us, tie us together, so that we will love each other to the extent that we will be tolerant, understanding, concerned one for the other and forgiving one another.

Another aspect of this relationship is one of sharing. My sister and I have shared all types of occasions, both happy and sad, good times and bad times, joys and sorrows. In reading 1 John, one of these times came to my mind so vividly, as John said, "By this we know love, that he (Christ) laid down his life for us; and we ought to lay down our lives for the brethren." There was an occasion when my sister literally put her life in jeopardy for me. Although she has angina, and had just had a bad cardiagram reading and several other complications, she came to me in my darkest hour. I am certain that, had she asked her doctor, he would have said, "No, you must not go." But she came, nevertheless, and stayed one month with me during a very trying time. I could not help thinking, when reading the Scripture in 1 John, how she demonstrated that love in the human family.

If we can just translate all these good attributes that are exhibited in our natural family relationships into our spiritual family, what an effective witness to the world we could be.

We are commanded to love one another. "Love one another from the heart fervently" I Peter 1:22. Jesus commands us to love one another in John 15:17; Paul also, In Romans 12:9-10, "Love one another with brotherly affection." When the New Testament speaks of "brethren," "brothers" and "brotherhood," the whole body of believers is intended, sisters included, of course. These Scriptures are certainly not meant to be exclusive, for we are to love all men; but there should be a special bond between blood-bought Christians, and it should be evident. 1 John is a reiteration, over and over again, of exhortation to love one another. In 1 John 3:14, we are told that this love is evidence that we have passed from darkness to light, from death to life. We are told that we are liars if we say that we love God and do not love our brother. If we say we know Christ and do not obey his commands, we are liars.

Do we really love one another? Let us apply the acid test—see some facets of love and some of the things that love is not. The passage from 1 Corinthians 13, which follows, is not new, but may be expressed in a little different language (my own). I think we need to look at this often, examine our lives, and see if these things are evident.

"Love is patient and kind, never jealous, or envious, or boastful, or proud; never conceited, selfish, rude, or ill-mannered; does not demand its own way; not irritable or touchy. Love does not hold grudges or keep a record of wrongs, will hardly notice when others do it wrong; does not gloat over other men's sins, not happy with evil; hates injustice, rejoices when truth wins out" (1 Corinthians 13:4-7).

"Dear Lord, we pray for a greater love for thee and for our sisters and brothers in Christ. Help us to manifest it in our attitude, and in our actions one toward the other. In Christ's name we pray. Amen."

—Inez Seabrook

FOR WOMEN, the love of sisters is basic to all fellowship in the body of Christ, and its characteristics are woven into other relationships. ARE THERE OTHER RELATIONSHIPS? IF SO, WHAT?

Remember that Jesus said, "Whoever does the will of my Father in heaven is my brother, and sister, and MOTHER." Women were designed to be, not only sisters, but mothers and grandmothers.

In our mobile society, many young Christian families find themselves far away from home ties, miles from mother and grandmother. There is a need for Christian women to step into this role and lend support, encouragement and counsel to the young wife and mother.

God saw such a need, for we read the following inspired instructions:

"Likewise, teach the older women to be reverent in the way they live, not to be slanderers or addicted to much wine, but to teach what is good. Then they can train the younger women to love their husbands and children, to be self controlled and pure, to be busy at home, to be kind, and to be subject to their husbands, so that no one will malign the word of God" (Titus 2:3-5 NIV).

Are our older women accepting their responsibility to train the younger? I am afraid that, too often, this duty is shirked with the excuse that teaching is not one's talent, or even with an unwillingness to accept the fact that one might be considered an "older woman." Our culture is probably too much attuned to staying young-looking, to a glorification of youth. We fail to consider the advantages of age and to teach its proper respect. But there is a wisdom that comes only from experience and a patience, tolerance and understanding that grows with age.

It was very refreshing to hear a friend of mine remark, "Since I have recently celebrated my 40th birthday, I am now numbered among the older women and it is time I started to teach the younger." A 40th birthday may not be the criterion for such a transition; but if a woman has been a Christian for 15 or 20 years and is not teaching or training younger women in *some manner*, she needs to examine her spiritual maturity and her commitment.

To "train" does not necessarily mean to teach a ladies class, although it certainly includes that. I doubt seriously if Paul had in mind a ladies class when he wrote this passage, for it means so much more than that. We *do*, in our society, need ladies classes, and we need more and more ladies, of all ages, who are willing to teach. But we also desperately need the one-to-one relationship of love and concern that can provide encouragement and help with specific problems.

As older women, are we providing this type of training? Or are we failing our younger women?

Can a younger woman find among us an example of spiritual maturity? Do our speech and actions show love for the Lord?

Do they see us as Christian examples, or as examples of materialism?

Do we show them concern, sympathy and understanding? Or do they see us as indifferent to their problems?

Do we seem too busy with our own affairs? Do they feel free to call on us? Do we make ourselves available?

Do we prove ourselves trustworthy? Or do they hear us talk about others to the extent that they would be afraid to confide in us?

Titus says that the older woman must live in such a way as to gain respect before she can train others. She must teach what is good by setting a high standard herself. Then the young woman is wise who seeks her companionship as a "second mother," to whom she can go for counsel and encouragement. It is only natural that we gravitate toward those of our own age and at the same stage in life and find our closest friends among them, but all of us are missing valuable assets to our growth and enrichment if we do not seek among our friends some of those who are both older and younger than we. Such a friendship can work a two-way blessing, as it may be the case that the older woman's children and grand-children live far away from her. Each will feel needed as they minister to the other; and, as they learn to love and understand each other better, they can talk more freely and counsel together on specific problems.

Generally speaking, many young wives of today are in anguish over how to handle the differences that crop up in the marriage relationship. Often adjustment in the sex-life is a problem. God's Word speaks to this problem, pointing to an unselfish love, based on mutual understanding and a desire to fulfill the other's need. Some women, finding the concept of submission difficult, may be helped by a study of its true meaning, as well as advice on encouraging the husband to take his God-given responsibility as head of the house.

Young or immature Christians have difficulty handling criticism, tending not only to be critical themselves, but to let the fear of criticism keep them from doing anything worthwhile. Mature Christians must set the example of rising above unwarranted criticism as well as the human tendency to be critical themselves—of *anyone*.

Young mothers and homemakers are often frustrated in trying to be "busy at home." Feeling tied down, with so many opportunities and activities beckoning in this modern society, they need to be constantly aware of the vast importance of motherhood and of its fleeting opportunities. When young mothers look with envy to those women whose children are grown and who have time to participate in things outside the home, they need encouragement for the "now" and the realization that the future can only be sweet if a woman has used well her time for rearing her children. There is a time for everything, and each time of life is to be lived to the fullest in all its privileges and responsibilities. Helen Young has so beautifuly penned this thought in her poem, "Babies Don't Wait," from which an excerpt appears at the close of this lesson.

If every Christian woman, young or old, will accept and make the most of each season of life, reaching out to her sister, sharing, encouraging, admonishing and showing a need for each other— being mother, daughter, grandmother, sister, as the occasion demands—then, truly, WE WILL BE THE FAMILY OF GOD.

Following excerpts from:
BABIES DON'T WAIT
—by Helen M. Young

There is a time to hold him close and tell him the sweetest story
   ever told;·
A time to show him God in earth and sky and flower, to teach him
   to wonder and reverence.
There is a time to leave the dishes, to swing in the park,
To run a race, to draw a picture, to catch a butterfly, to give him
   happy comradeship.
There is a time to point the way, to teach his infant lips to pray,
To teach his heart to love God's word, to love God's day,
For babies don't wait.

There is a time to sing instead of grumble, to smile instead of frown,
To kiss away the tears and laugh at broken dishes,
A time to share with him my best in attitudes—a love of life, a love
   of God, a love of family.
There is a time to answer his questions, all his questions,
Because there may come a time when he will not want my answers.
There is a time to teach him so patiently to obey, to put his toys away.
There is a time to teach him the beauty of duty, the habit of Bible
   study, the joy of worship at home, the peace of prayer,
For children won't wait.

There is a time to treasure every fleeting minute of his childhood,
Just eighteen precious years to inspire and train him.
I will not exchange this birthright for a mess of pottage called social
   position, or business or professional reputation, or a pay check.
An hour of concern today may save years of heartache tomorrow,
The house will wait, the dishes will wait, the ironing will wait,
A new car can wait, a new carpet can wait, a new room can wait,
But children don't wait.

There will be a time when there will be no slamming of doors, no
toys on the stairs, no childhood quarrels, no fingerprints on the
wallpaper.
Then may I look back with joy and not regret.
There will be a time to concentrate on service outside my home;
On visiting the sick, the bereaved, the discouraged, the untaught;
To give myself to the "least of these."
There will be a time to look back and know that these years of
motherhood were not wasted.

I pray there will be a time to see him an upright and an honest man,
loving God and serving all.
God, give me wisdom to see that today is my day with my children.
That there is no unimportant moment in their lives.
May I know that no other career is so precious,
No other work so rewarding,
No other task so urgent.
May I not defer it nor neglect it,
But by thy Spirit accept it gladly, joyously, and by thy grace realize
That the time is short and my time is now,
For babies won't wait!

Reprinted by permission of author

FOR DISCUSSION:

1. What is involved in training the younger women? What are
   their needs? How can we help?
2. Who is the older woman? Where do *I* fit into the picture?
   What are *my* responsibilities?
3. How does an older woman show herself as being available
   and willing to listen?
4. Have a panel, composed of both younger and older women, to
   discuss the needs of each and ways of being closer spiritual
   sisters, better mothers and daughters in the family of God.

FOOTNOTES:

1. Frederick B. Speakman, *The Salty Tang* (Old Tappan, NJ: Fleming H. Revell
   Co., 1954), p. 31.
2. William Barclay, *The Gospel of Matthew, Vol. 2* (Philadelphia: Westminster
   Press), p. 59. *The Gospel of Mark* (Philadelphia: Westminster Press), pp. 78-79.

LESSON 9:
Inner Spirituality

**"Do you not see that whatever goes into a man
from outside cannot defile him?"** Mark 7:18

LESSON SCRIPTURE: Mark 7:14-23
OTHER SCRIPTURES: Galations 2:20   John 15:4, 5
Colossians 1:26, 27   Ephesians 3:16, 17
2 Corinthians 4:16, 17   Ephesians 4:23, 24
2 Corinthians 5:17   1 Peter 1:23
Romans 7:15; 8:9   John 3:5

To follow Jesus, to call him Lord and Master, is to be possessed
of a glowing heart. Constantly, as in this passage in Mark 7, Jesus
is trying to teach the secret of the *inward glow*. Repeatedly,
however, we let our old natural selves and our busy, everyday
human affairs dull our hearing.

"Are you also without understanding?" Jesus exclaimed to his
disciples as he attempted to focus their attention inwardly to
the heart. "Do you not see that whatever goes into a man from
outside cannot defile him . . . but what comes out of a man is
what defiles a man." His words had fallen on the unresponsive
ears of the Pharisees also, as they were too concerned with eating
and with the ceremonial washing of hands to understand. It was
their complaint that the disciples of Jesus were not complying with
this tradition which caused Jesus to issue them a sharp rebuke as
well as a valuable lesson.

We realize that the washing of hands under question here was not
merely to cleanse the hands of grime and dirt before one ate, but a
ceremonial tradition to which the Pharisees complied meticulously.
According to Alfred Edersheim, a noted authority on Jewish custom,
this practice was admitted to be not a part of the law of Moses but
of the tradition of the elders. Nevertheless, to neglect it was to be
guilty of "gross carnal defilement and could lead to temporal
destruction." Since it was a ceremony of purification, the water

must not have been used for any other purpose, lest it be defiled; consequently, large vessels or jars stored that which was fit for use. A specified amount of water was poured on both hands, which must be free of anything covering them. In order to be sure that the whole hand was washed and that the water polluted by the hand did not run down again, the hands were lifted up to make the water run to the wrist—if the water remained short of the wrist, the hands were not considered clean.

These minute details may look rather ridiculous to us, but to the Pharisees they were sacred. Jesus rebuked them, saying, "You have a fine way of rejecting the commandment of God, in order to keep your tradition!" We know that Jesus kept the law perfectly, but some of his most scathing remarks were directed against the traditions of the Jews. There is a warning here to us, lest we encumber our Christianity with needless and unauthorized traditions and neglect to take every precaution to keep the heart, and the life, pure.

Jesus assures his disciples that the things that defile a man are those things that come from within, from the heart; for the sinful actions which condemn first originate in the heart. They come out of what one is—mind, thoughts, inmost self. Be assured that there is no evil outside a person, real or imagined, that can separate him from God except that evil which is in his heart!

We understand that the word "heart" is used by biblical writers to indicate, not the emotions, but the entire personality—one's own central self. This includes the whole of the thought-world, and how important is the inward world of thoughts! It is this that distinguishes me as a woman, in contrast to machines—in fact, this is what I am! And with all that I am, I am called to love God! True spirituality lies in the realm of the thought-world, for the reality of communion with God must take place there. We can read God's Word, pray, even call ourselves communing by partaking of the Lord's Supper, but if our minds are far away, if our thoughts are not on what we are doing, there is no communion.

Since the thought-world is all-important (Jesus saying that only that which proceeds from it can condemn), let us explore this thought-world to see what is included, what does proceed from it and why. A psychological treatise is not intended here, nor is it within our capabilities; we are seeking only a simple understanding.

The word "thoughts" in verse 21 of the text translates a Greek word that includes both what a man is thinking and what he plans to do. You will appreciate the fact that I can sit in my easy chair all day and think about cleaning my house, but unless I make the decision to get up and do something about it, my house will never be clean. More importantly, I can learn about Jesus and believe in my mind that He is the Son of God, but unless I decide to become a Christian, I will never be one. Our thought-world, then, includes more than just thinking; it includes, at least, deciding or choosing.

Life is made up of a series of choices. The choice I make today is based largely on the choice I made yesterday, and with each choice I am progressing either toward God or away. Taking life as a whole, with all its innumerable choices, I can slowly turn into a person in harmony with God or into one in disharmony with the entire purpose of existence.

If choices and decisions are so important, how are they made in my thought-world? What is it about myself that causes me to come to a certain decision? How do I choose between different courses of action?

We are all swayed at times by outside influences. But the final choice is made; a firm decision is reached as a result of my motives, my purposes or direction in life, my conviction. Consider for a moment a simple diagram, such as the following:

THOUGHTS
———————

MOTIVES   CHOICES   ACTIONS
&
DECISIONS

Whatever my motives are, they color or influence all thoughts, decisions and actions. For instance, if I am a very selfish person, what I think and what I choose to do will be colored by my selfishness. The right motive can color an action beautiful, while the wrong motive colors it black. Let me illustrate. Suppose that, as you grieve over the death of your father, you are surprised to see a mere acquaintance at the funeral home to pay respects. You would probably think, "How very thoughtful of someone I have known so little. What a beautiful act of love and concern!" If however, a few weeks later you learn that this person has become affiliated with an insurance firm and wishes to call on you as a salesman, you begin to question his motive in establishing previous contact with you. What looked like a beautiful act of kindness could become an ugly thing, if done for business advantage.

What we do is evidence of what we are only if our motives are honest and pure. That is why only God can judge a person's actions, because only He can look into the heart and know the motive. Since man judges on outward appearances, he can be fooled by an outward act which may be a sham or a cover. But what about a spontaneous act or spur-of-the-moment reaction? Is the truth what pops out before one has time to put on a disguise? Is what a person does when he is taken off guard the best evidence for what sort of person he is?

Our actions spring from what we *really* are in our inner selves. As a free person, I can control my thoughts and choices; I am responsible for my actions. But I find it very difficult to change my motives. I strongly desire to be always a loving person; but I know, as a matter of practical experience, that I often act from selfish motives, not from love. Perhaps it is true of most of us that our behavior is not always what we would like it to be. Paul expressed our dilemma in Romans 7:15-8:1 (Phillips).

My own behavior baffles me. For I find myself not doing what I really want to do but doing what I really loathe . . . I often find that I have the will to do good, but not the power. That is, I don't accomplish the good I set out to do, and the evil I don't really want to do I find I am always doing . . . In my mind I am God's willing servant, but in my own nature I am bound fast, as I say, to the law of sin and death. It is an agonizing situation, and who on earth can set me free from the clutches of my sinful nature? *I thank God there is a way out through Jesus Christ our Lord.* No condemnation now hangs over the head of those who are "in" Christ Jesus. For the new spiritual principle of life "in" Christ Jesus lifts me out of the old vicious circle of sin and death.

If we are in Christ Jesus, He has taken possession of us. And if He is to take possession, it must be in this central self where the direction of the will, the motives and purposes, determine behavior. If He is reigning there by the power of His spirit, all the rest of our nature must come under His influence. Since our actions spring from what we really are in our inner selves, it is of the utmost importance that we define honestly to ourselves our purpose and direction in life and tie our motives down in a deep conviction to live for the Lord. Someone has said that conviction is information you have gathered, examined and tied down securely within yourself so that it becomes a part of you. Then that conviction influences all your thoughts, decisions and actions. What you say and do comes naturally, from this conviction.

Going back to the suggested diagram, picture in your mind encircling the motives with a strong cord, tieing it down securely. This cord represents a deep conviction to hand over one's will to God, and to purpose to live for Him. Such a diagram may be crude and oversimplified, but perhaps it will help us see the all-encompassing effect of having Christ at the center of our being. A deep conviction to serve God wholeheartedly means a Christ-controlled nature, and only this can give us the inward glow. For what we do, NATURALLY, is evidence of what we are, GENUINELY.

We can easily see this principle demonstrated in nature—why not in ourselves?

"Sometime ago I took time to look a red rose fully in the face. It was possessed of a beauty that had power to lift the heart and set the soul to dreaming. But after I had looked at this flower for a moment I said, 'You may relax now. You can't go on being that beautiful all of the time—it would give you a nervous breakdown!' But the rose only smiled and said, 'I am not putting on a show. I look like this all of the time. It is my nature.' Recently, while walking in a forest, I came on a mockingbird in concert. This artist was singing as if practicing for an appearance in heaven. After I had listened quite a while, I stepped out from behind a tree and said, 'You may rest your voice now. There is nobody here but me. There is no need for you to exert yourself so strenuously just for one.' But the mockingbird said, 'I didn't know you were here. You see, it is natural for me to sing as I do.'

"When I visited Mount Shasta one day and saw it stabbing the clouds and wrapping a mantel of eternal whiteness around its shoulders, I asked how it managed to climb so far toward the stars. 'It must be a terrible strain,' I concluded. 'Oh no,' it replied, 'It is as easy for me to be tall as for a molehill to be low.' So it is! In the same way, it is as easy for a giant redwood to climb to a height of 300 feet as for a toadstool to hug the ground . . . . Niagra finds it just as easy to crash with thunder as a wet-weather rivulet to evaporate in silence."[1]

In the variations of nature, each possesses a beauty in what it is by nature, in what it does naturally. This is true of human beings also. The lovely soprano, Beverly Sills, demonstrates an innate ability to trill beautiful arias with seemingly little effort. If most of us struggled with those mountainous high C's, it would be a disaster. Singing, to be beautiful, must not be too marked by strain.

There must be a spontaneity of goodness—a lack of strain—also, for Christianity to be attractive. To be grandly good without, in a sense, trying—this is what it means to take on the nature of the inward glow. This is why God has given us a new nature so that our goodness and Christlikeness can come, naturally, from within.

You may think, "Well, you really have your head in the clouds now, because I'm just not that Christlike." I assure you that none of us is, by our old nature. "Put off your old nature," said Paul to the Ephesians, "which belongs to your former manner of life and is corrupt through deceitful lusts, and be renewed in the spirit of your minds, and put on the new nature, created after the likeness of God in true righteousness and holiness" (Ephesians 4:22-24).

When we realize the new nature we as Christians have, and when we operate on faith, nourishing it and allowing it to grow and mature, Christlikeness can come naturally. Is this not what Christianity is all about?

All through the New Testament letters we read that Christians
are "born again" people, that Christ "is formed" in us—living
in us; we read about "having the mind" of Christ. Surely this means
more than something merely mental or moral; it means more than
reading what Jesus said and trying to do it. We understand that by
Christ's indwelling spirit, He is killing off my old nature and
making over my nature into the kind of nature he has, into a
Christlike nature. Of course, in this process I am not passive. I
can quench the spirit and stunt spiritual growth or I can yeild myself
in obedience, nourish and feed the spirit, and thus stimulate growth.
A beautiful nature will not be mine overnight, but is a growth
process, as is my physical life.

My natural life is not something I have on my own. I
am living and breathing today because my parents gave me life. I
can abuse this body; I can starve it; I can even kill it by committing
suicide. Also, I can nourish it; I can feed it; I can exercise it; I can
provide the atmosphere in which it can grow to its potential. But,
whatever I do to this body, it is still something that I did not get
on my own. In the same way, this Christ-life within us is from God.
Even the best Christian that ever lived is only nourishing and
feeding the life that God gave him. And this has some very practical
consequences.[2]

As our natural bodies have a tendency to heal themselves, I can
cut or I can hurt my body, but if I give it enough time, it can, to a
certain extent, heal itself. And so with this Christlife within us. The
Christian is not a person who doesn't stumble and fall, who doesn't
make mistakes and doesn't sin. This Christlife within enables us to
pick ourselves up and to start over again. It is easy to see that as a
Christian we are in so much better position than a person who is
trying on his own to be good.

When Paul, in Romans 7, described the dilemma of human nature
to which we alluded earlier, he furnished the answer, the marvelous
solution, in the next chapter:

"Those who live according to their sinful nature have their
minds set on what that nature desires; but those who live in
accordance with the Spirit have their minds set on what the
Spirit desires. The mind of sinful man is death, but the mind
controlled by the Spirit is life and peace . . . You, however, are
controlled not by your sinful nature but by the Spirit, if the
Spirit of God lives in you. *And if anyone does not have the
Spirit* of Christ, he does not belong to Christ" (Romans 8:5,
6, 9 NIV).

God has put into His creatures a little of Himself—a little of
his reasoning power; that is how we think, choose and decide. But
Christians have the additional advantage that "God's love has been

poured into our hearts through the Holy Spirit which has been given us" (Romans 5:5).

When Jesus said to the disciples, "Don't you see that whatever goes into a man from outside does not defile him?" they did not understand any more than did the Pharisees. But you and I, knowing what we now know of the inward self (even though we do not understand it completely), have an insight into the meaning of His words and the blessed privilege of experiencing the new birth and the new life. We can know as a reality the words of Jesus, when he told Nicodemus, "I tell you the truth, unless a man is born of water and the Spirit, he cannot enter the kingdom of God. Flesh gives birth to flesh, but the Spirit gives birth to spirit" (John 3:5 NIV).

As Francis Schaeffer pointed out in *True Spirituality,* there is no entrance into spiritual life except through the door of spiritual birth, just as there is no way to begin physical life except through physical birth. One must become a Christian by being born of both water and the spirit, in the watery grave of baptism, before she can know anything of true spirituality. The new birth is necessary as a beginning, but we must realize *it is only the beginning.* (See Acts 2:38-42 and Romans 6:3-11.)

However, it is a sad commentary on human nature that so many people have experienced the new birth but have failed to nourish and feed the inner man. Once we have accepted Christ, we must hold before our minds *each day* some of God's word, and we must constantly seek His will. We have to be continually reminded of our belief or it will not remain alive—it must be fed. Daily prayer, Bible reading, religious and devotional books, Bible study groups, worship periods—all these are important and necessary for the growth of inner spirituality. Just as important is the elimination of the wrong kind of reading and viewing. We should be even more careful about what we put into our minds than we are about what we put into our stomachs. As digestive upsets quickly follow the eating of spoiled food, so mental and spiritual upsets follow from feeding the mind the wrong things.

The inner glow is also brightened or dulled by our choice of companionship. "How much we owe to our fellow believers! There are those in whose presence it is easy to doubt. But there are also those in whose presence it is easy to believe the highest and the best. When my own lamp of faith has burned low, I have gone again and again to relight it at the glowing torches of some of the choice believers whom I have known along the way."[3]

"From within," said Jesus, "out of men's hearts come the evil things that make a man unclean." True spirituality is not just outward, it is inward. It begins with the new birth; but this is only the beginning, just as physical birth is only the beginning of our physical lives. After we are born, the important thing is the living of our lives in all their relationships, developing our God-given talents. The important thing after being born spiritually is to live in the proper relationship to God and others, and to let that inner glow permeate our every action.

FOR FURTHER STUDY AND DISCUSSION:

1. What precedes or is involved in each of my actions? Is it thought? choice? decision? motive? purpose? (Consider the importance of each of these and what control you have over them.)
2. What do these New Testament expressions mean to me and for my life?
   "Christ lives in me" (Galatians 2:20; Colossians 1:26, 27; John 15:4, 5)
   "the inner man" (2 Corinthians 4:16, 17; Ephesians 3:16, 17)
   "the new nature" (2 Corinthians 5:17; Ephesians 4:23, 24)
3. If, as Christians, we are not producing the fruit we should, can you give any reasons why?
4. Perhaps the greatest evidence to a woman that she is a Christian may be seen in her change of character. As you reflect on your life, name two areas which have been undergoing change.
5. Discuss the value of reading religious and devotional literature in addition to Bible study. Share with each other the type of reading and books which have proved to be most helpful.

FOOTNOTES:

1. Clovis Chappell, *Living Zestfully* (Nashville: Abingdon-Cokesbury Press, 1959), pp. 28-29.
2. C.S. Lewis, *The Best of C.S. Lewis*
3. Clovis Chappell, *Questions Jesus Asked* (Nashville: Abingdon Press: renewal 1976), p. 43.

LESSON 10:
Seeking Approval
by Jan Thomas

"How can you believe if you accept praise from one another, yet make no effort to obtain the praise that comes from the only God?" John 5:44 NIV

LESSON SCRIPTURE: John 5:39-44
OTHER SCRIPTURES:

Mark 12:31	Matthew 5:11-12	Philippians 2:5-11
Galatians 6:3	John 15:18-19	1 Corinthians 15:10
Romans 12:3	Matthew 5:16	Ephesians 2:10
John 7:13	Galatians 1:10	Romans 5:6-8
2 Corinthians 10:12	Romans 3:20, 21-22	2 Timothy 1:7-8
John 12:42-43	John 14:6	Romans 1:16
Matthew 6:2, 5	Romans 2:29	Mark 8:38
Matthew 6:16	John 12:26	Romans 7:14-8:11
Matthew 23:5-12	Romans 8:29	Matthew 26:69-75
Mark 7:5-13	Galatians 3:27	Daniel 6
Mark 12:38-40	Colossians 1:19-20	
Matthew 10:22	Matthew 6:1, 16, 17	

Wanting Approval in Our Lives

Who among us can truthfully say that he seeks approval from no one? Who can honestly say "I don't care what anyone thinks of me"? We may not call it approval—we may use honor, praise or glory, but in some way, each of us basically wants recognition and approval.

Not living to ourselves, we are involved with other human beings right from birth, and at every state in our lives approval is sought. Approval at a young age is translated by children as love, and each in his own way tries to gain this love, first from parents. A graphic example involves efforts to toilet train a 2-year-old. How excited the

87

parents become when the child is successful, and how the child basks in the hearty praise he receives!

As he grows older, he not only wants approval and acceptance from his parents but from his peers as well. We adults can surely recall participating in the agonies and frustrations of interpersonal relationships in those pre-adolescent and early teen years. How tremendously important it becomes to be accepted and approved by one's friends! And often we retain this desire as adults. Most of us mellow a little as we grow older, and we learn to cope with ourselves and our relationships, yet this desire for approval from our fellowman remains.

Some "adult" levels of this desire for praise surface in the use of our talents. And God in His wisdom has given us a variety of different talents, just as we have different physical measurements. Since we mentioned measurements, how many of us have ever felt "fat"? Whether we really are or not, how do we act and feel? Do we want to wear something snug or something that would call attention to our appearance, or do we wear something loose, something in which we won't really be noticed by other people? On the other hand, when we've been on a diet and lost weight, or if we know our figure looks pretty good anyway, don't we want to wear things that are close-fitting or that will show off our figure to the best advantage?

Aren't we this way with our talents, too? If we're good cooks, we want to be known for it; if we sew well, we want to be known as a seamstress; if we're good teachers, we want all to recognize us as such; if we're shrewd businesswomen, we want our colleagues to recognize and acknowledge this.

Another area affected by our need for approval is that of good deeds or good works. Most of us do a great many things for other people, both Christians and non-Christians. Yet don't we want at least someone to know that we did a certain thing? Don't we find ourselves mentioning, just in passing conversation, some particular thing that we've done for someone, so that someone is aware of the deed?

Interwoven with the individual's concern for the approval of others is the encompassing need for self-approval. William Shakespeare gave us the familiar phrase "To thine own self be true." We are often encouraged by psychologists to develop a sense of our own self-worth, and not to lean too heavily on others. Our Lord himself taught in Mark 12:31, "You shall love your neighbor as yourself." Even though we might feel very self-reliant, we might look at sources of our self-approval. Sociologist Charles Horton Cooley proposed that individuals exhibit what he calls the "looking-glass self." He stated that our self-concept is formed by (1) our imagination of how we are to others, (2) our imagination of their judgment of how we are, and (3) our feelings about that judgment. With maturity, we can change our reference frame so that some groups' judgment about us are given greater significance than others.[1] Our self-concept is deeply involved with the desire for approval and praise. Paul gives Christians warnings in this area in Romans 12:3, 2 Corinthians 10:12 and Galatians 6:3, as he cautions us not to think of ourselves more highly than we ought.

This self-concept of ours is also influenced by our fear of disapproval. Early followers of Jesus were silent for fear of the Jews (John 7:13). Some Jewish leaders would not confess Jesus for fear of rejection (John 12:42-43). What are our feelings today about talking to friends, neighbors and associates about Jesus? Do we recognize in ourselves some of the fear of disapproval in this area?

A Look at Bible Personalities

There are two outstanding Bible personalities who seem to demonstrate some lessons for us here. The exemplary figure, one who must have been a joy to God, was Daniel. We recall how he was miraculously delivered from the lions' mouths. No fear of man's disapproval is in evidence here in his unyielding devotion to God and his commands. On the other hand, there is Peter on the night that Jesus was arrested. In Matthew 26:69-75 and the three parallel accounts in Mark, Luke and John, we see the man who just hours earlier had assured the Lord that he would go to prison and even die with him deny three times that he even knew Jesus because of what some strangers might think. How often do we find ourselves Peters instead of Daniels!

Jesus' Teachings About the Desire for Approval

Jesus, during his brief ministry, had much to say about our values in seeking glory from men. He condemned the Pharisees and hypocrites on many occasions: for desiring honor from men as a motive for giving to the needy and for prayer; for fasting as a show, loving praise from men; for vain worship and traditions of men; for loving to be greeted in the market-place. (See Matthew 6:2, 5, 16; 23:5-12; Mark 7:5-13; 12:38-40.) In fact, he was careful to point out that those who were His disciples would get negative reactions from people in the world. He taught in Matthew 10:22 and John 15:18-19 that Christians will be hated, that we will be persecuted and slandered by men, yet blessed by God.

The Lord went further in His teaching about the world's praise and directed any praise from the Christian's life and works to the Father. "In the same way, let your light shine before men, that they may see your good deeds and praise your Father in heaven"

(Matthew 5:16 NIV). "Be careful not to do your 'acts of righteousness' before men, to be seen by them. If you do, you will have no reward from your Father in heaven" (Matthew 6:1). (see also Matthew 6:16, 17.)

Seeking Approval from God

Paul tells us in Galatians 1:10 that servants of Christ are not trying to please men. We are to direct our efforts for praise and glory to our Father who sees and knows all that we do. As Christians we do seek God's approval. We want very much to be accepted by our Father. Yet often we are misdirected in these efforts by trying to keep the Law, or go by a set of rules and earn "points." Paul's words in Romans 3:20 make these efforts futile, for "no one will be declared righteous in his sight by observing the law" (NIV). Reading further in verses 21 and 22 we find that our relationship to God is through Christ. Jesus teaches in John 14:6 that no one comes to the Father except through Him.

The marvelous part of God's plan is not that we earn His favor by our own merit but that when we believe and accept His Son and commit our lives to Him and receive circumcision by the Spirit (Romans 2:29) we receive praise from God. In John 12:26 Jesus revealed that the Father will honor those who serve Him. Those who are justified are glorified (Romans 8:29, 30). Glory, acceptance, approval and praise from God were focused on his Son (Colossians 1:19-20); so when we have the mind of Christ, we share in His glory (Galatians 3:27). We can then demonstrate the same attitude which Christ had as described in Philippians 2:5-11, in which all his glory was directed to God.

Applications to Our Lives

Looking at our everyday lives, what do these teachings mean for us? We have so many natural tendencies which seem to be basic to all individuals. We base our self-concept on approval of others; we want someone to know of our good works; we want feelings of self-worth in relation to worldly standards, and we tend to avoid things that might cause disapproval or ridicule from others. This is the way we are when we are on our own.

But, praise God, life in Christ changes these natural tendencies! Life in the Son, lived by the power of God's Spirit, brings drastic changes into our world. Our talents are now used with open recognition and praise to God, the Creator and Giver of all talents. "But by the grace of God, I am what I am . . ." (1 Corinthians 15:10). Our good works are done to glorify God, not ourselves. "For we are God's workmanship, created in Christ Jesus to do good works, which God prepared in advance for us to do" (Ephesians 2:10 NIV). "Let your light shine before men, that they may see your good deeds and praise your Father in heaven" (Matthew 5:16 NIV). Our feelings of self-worth are based on God's marvelous love for us, not what others of our family or friends or anyone else may think of us. "You see, at just the right time, when we were still powerless, Christ died for the ungodly. Very rarely will anyone die for a righteous man, though for a good man someone might possibly dare to die. But God demonstrates his own love for us in this: While we were still sinners, Christ died for us" (Romans 5:6-8 NIV). Our fears of disapproval are overcome—we are not ashamed of Christ or His gospel, and His spirit gives us love and power and self-control (Mark 8:38; Romans 1:16; 2 Timothy 1:7-8).

It would be easy for us to recognize our weaknesses and our natural tendencies, and to say that it's just the way we are, that if these desires are basic God must have made us the way we are, that we can't help our feelings and desires. But no. Ours is truly the victory over human nature left alone to run its course without the direction and guidance of its Creator. Paul describes our situation so perfectly in Romans 7:14-8:11. The conflict between what we are and what we can be is resolved if we but let the Master take over.

We can finally ask ourselves the question Jesus asked the Jews: "How can you believe if you accept praise from one another, yet make no effort to obtain the praise that comes from the only God?"

QUESTIONS FOR DISCUSSION OR THOUGHT:

1. What are the special talents God has given me? How can I use these talents in a way that will bring praise to Him instead of praise to me?
2. How would I feel about doing my good deeds in secret, never mentioning them or anything about them to anyone else? How can I do good works so that anyone who does see them will give glory to God?
3. What holds me back from discussing Jesus freely with my friends and neighbors?

FOOTNOTES:

1. Horton and Hunt, *Sociology* (New York: McGraw-Hill, 1964), pp. 99-101, 116.

LESSON 11:
Sin and Suffering

"Do you think that these Galileans were worse sinners than all the other Galileans, because they suffered thus?"

Luke 13:2

LESSON SCRIPTURE: Luke 13:2-5
OTHER SCRIPTURES: John 9:1-3   2 Corinthians 5:1-4
Psalms 34:4, 46:1-2   Philippians 4:13, 19
Romans 8:28   Ephesians 6:13
Isaiah 26:3   Matthew 11:28-29
Proverbs 3:5

"Certain individuals had just rushed into the presence of Jesus bearing tragic tidings of how these Galileans had come to worship, but had ended by having their own blood mingled with the blood of the beasts that they were offering in sacrifice. What terrible sinners they must have been! That is what they meant to imply as they told their heavy news.

"But Jesus did not agree with them. Instead he told them frankly that this tragedy did not indicate that these slaughtered saints were worse than their fellows. If you and I are in an automobile accident and you are killed and I escape, that does not argue that you were wicked while I am good. Instead of agreeing with these men Jesus affirmed that they themselves were just as real sinners as those who suffered."[1]

The problem of pain and suffering is one that men have struggled with through the ages. Since it is one that is ever present with us, and that all of us have to face to some degree, no study of values would be complete without a consideration of it. Let me urge you to study carefully the following exposition on *Sin and Suffering,* by Gayle Reaves, for I am sure you will find it to be a Christian viewpoint, and therefore extremely helpful.

93

Then let us also not forget the reply of Jesus to these men. What did our Lord have to say? He called them to repentance for they were *all* sinners just as we are sinners. If we meet suffering within his will, victory is ours!

Sin and Suffering
By Gayle Reaves

Luke 13:2-5 contains a question faced by our Lord. "Now there were some present at that time who told Jesus about the Galilaeans whose blood Pilate had mixed with their sacrifices. Jesus answered, 'Do you think that these Galileans were worse sinners than all the other Galileans because they suffered this way?' I tell you, no! But unless you repent, you too will all perish" (NIV).

Is there some reason for man's suffering? Does it serve some good purpose? Why disease and death?

Pain and suffering are all around us. No one goes through life escaping it in many forms. The daily newspapers and newscasts are evidence that our world is faced hourly with the staggering problem of suffering. "Man comes into this world with a cry of pain and leaves with a sigh."[2] Pain can be a gradual thing or it can be sudden. It can be self-induced, often unconsciously, or a result of carelessness. "It is seldom announced—always unwanted."[3] I think our frequent question is "Why does this have to happen?"

C. S. Lewis, who was at one time an atheist, became a believer in Christ and a defender of Christianity. In his book "The Problem of Pain," he includes the question, "If God were good, He would wish to make His creatures perfectly happy, and if God' were almighty, He would be able to do what He wished. But the creatures are not happy. Therefore God lacks either goodness, or power, or both?" Is there an answer to this question?

"When God created man, he made him a creature with freedom of choice and freedom of will. When God chose to make man a creature of freedom, an inevitable result was that man could choose evil as well as good. So when man chooses to love God, it has real significance. But with this freedom of choice is included the possibility of choosing evil as well as good. Because man has freedom of will, there have been mistakes, blunders, and wrong choices. The events of history and the state of the present world show ample evidence of the fact that man has often chosen wrongly and has suffered as a result."[3] The sin of a nation often produces much suffering.

Suffering is often, but not always, a result of man's own sin. The Jews rigidly connected sin and suffering. We see in the book of Job that Job's friends were telling him to "Get everything right, Job, and you will be o.k." and that "God is really punishing you less than you deserve," but we see that Job was not being punished for anything. His answer was, "I don't really understand God, but I am going to trust him." This is the attitude we must take today, if we are to find peace and answers to our troubles.

In Exodus 15:26, God told the Israelites, "If thou wilt diligently hearken to the voice of the Lord thy God, and wilt do that which is right in his sight, and wilt give ear to his commandments, and keep all his statutes, I will put none of these diseases upon thee" (KJV). Was God saying that if we do right in his sight that we will not be punished by illness or disease, by pain or suffering? No, he was saying to his people that he was giving them rules and guidelines by which to go which were for their own well-being. Isn't that true for what he has given us today? Even without Christianity, even if we had no hope of eternal life with God after death, isn't the plan God has given for our life the very best plan for living at peace with ourselves and mankind? Isn't God's way best? Dr. Wm. Sadler, a psychiatrist, wrote, "The sincere acceptance of the principles and teachings of Christ with respect to the life of mental peace and joy, the life of unselfish thought and clean living, would at once wipe out more than half the difficulties, disease, and sorrows of the human race. Irrespective of the future rewards of living, laying aside all discussion of future life, it would pay any man or woman to live the Christ life just for the mental and moral rewards it affords here in this present world. Some day man may awake to the fact that the teachings of Christ are potent and powerful in preventing and curing disease. Some day our boasted scientific development, as regards mental and moral improvement, may indeed catch up with the teachings of the Man of Galilee."[5]

God gave the Israelites rules by which to go and it was not until hundreds of years later that medical science proved very sound reasons for some of these rules. One example was the eating of animal fat in Leviticus 7:22-24. Even though this is not a law for us today, research has shown the dangers of too much animal fat in our diets and the connection with cholesterol and arteriosclerosis. Another example is God's commandment to Abraham to circumcise Isaac on the 8th day of life. Hundreds of years later, medical science has found that the Vitamin K and other bloodclotting factors are highest in infants on the 7th and 8th day after birth. It has been found that cervical cancer is almost non-existent among Jewish women, and has now been discovered that circumcision plays an important part in the absence of this type cancer—a commandment by God to the Israelites.

Science is linking certain types of sinful habits to other diseases. The most common one is smoking, which is recognized as a cause of lung cancer and heart disease. People spend hundreds of dollars for their treatment of illnesses caused by the chemicals in tobacco, but so often are unable to give up the habit causing the problem. The sin of the addiction to alcohol causes suffering. It causes broken homes, heartache, loss of work and income, hungry children. It destroys healthy minds and bodies.

What about our sexually promiscuous society? It has caused veneral disease. Gonorrhea is one of the leading causes of blindness and syphilis is the greatest cause of infant death. We see here that obedience to just one of God's laws would completely wipe out the disease of VD. Often, the promiscuous teenager suffers from more than just VD, though. There is unwanted pregnancy, abortion, loss of self-respect, guilt and other emotional problems in later life.

Then, what about the sins of the mind? Anger, malice, self-centeredness, convetousness—all of the old nature—which we are commanded to put away (Galatians 5:19-24). These emotions are clearly recognized by psychiatrists as causes or aggravations of the majority of all diseases. One psychiatrist has said that the basic cause of unhappiness and mental illness, whatever the patient's complaints or his symptoms are, are rooted in his inability to love. "Love is as essential to happiness and mental health as food is to our physical being," said Dr. McMillan in None of these Diseases. "The cure for all the ills and wrongs, and the crimes of humanity all lie in one word—love."[6] Have you ever been around someone who was absolutely miserable with life? Think. There is in nearly every case, an obstacle in their capacity for love. Underneath the surface in this person are emotions of hate, anger, revenge, jealousy and on and on, completely destroying them. We should be encouraged to get our mental and spiritual and emotional selves more in tune with God's to enjoy better health and peace of mind.

We do not realize how important our emotional centers are. Our reaction to stress produces changes in all our mechanisms. It changes the amount of blood flow to our organs, it affects the secretions of certain glands, it changes the tension of muscles. Worry, stress and fatigue go hand in hand. We see after a day of much concern and anxiety, how exhausted we become, even more so than after a day of physical work. The cure for this is often physical work. Our emotional systems are much better off with a good leaf raking job or bathroom scrubbing than to sit and brood, and build up those unhealthy tensions. Prayer is a powerful and effective worry-remover. We cannot pray and worry at the same time. When we learn to pray with childlike sincerety, literally talking to and communing with God, we are in possession of the greatest secret, knowing that he cares for us. A clear conscience is the greatest barricade against mental problems.[7] He is the greatest physician.

J. C. Penney, in the crash of 1929, suffered great and almost fatal depression. His business was solid, but he had made some unwise personal commitments. He became ill and was hospitalized with sedatives, but no relief. His depression and mental state became worse and he was overtaken with the fear of death. He wrote farewell letters to his wife and son, because he did not expect to live until morning. The next morning, at his lowest hour, he heard singing in the hospital chapel and managed to pull himself together and entered as a group was singing "God will take care of you." After a scripture and a prayer, Mr. Penney said that something miraculous happened. He felt that he had been lifted out of darkness; he felt the power of God as he had never felt it before. He came to the realization that he alone was responsible for his troubles, and that God with his love was there to help him, and he could pull out of this. He said that from that day on, his life was free from worry. "God will take care of you."

Some of man's suffering is completely out of his hands. Some is due to the natural law of the universe. When God created the universe, he established the system with its natural laws, but sometimes in the process of nature, there is an occasional by-product or side effect. The same rains which are essential to our existense and to the beauty of our earth, also, under different conditions, take homes from their foundations and cost man his life and livelihood. Storms, floods, conditions that were orginally in the balance of nature, cause problems and suffering when this balance is upset. So with all of this, we must look beyond immediate concerns, no matter how serious or critical, to the master plan, God's plan for the human race, his *ultimate* goal for us.[8]

John 9:1-3 records a familiar passage concerning suffering. "As he (Jesus) passed by, he saw a man blind from his birth. And his disciples asked him 'Rabbi, who sinned, this man or his parents, that he was born blind?' Jesus answered, 'It was not that this man sinned, or his parents, but that the works of God might be made manifest.' " Did Jesus say that this man's affliction came to him to give an opportunity of showing what God can do? Affliction, sorrow, pain, disappointment, loss, always enable any man to show what God can do. When trouble and disaster fall upon a man who does not know God, then that man may well collapse, with no one to turn to, but when they fall on a man who lives and walks with God, they bring out strength and endurance. William Barclay tells of an old saint, who when he was dying, sent for his family, saying "Come and see how a Christian can die." He says that it is when life hits us a terrible blow that we can show the world how a Christian can live, and if need be, die. He relates that any kind of suffering is a God-given opportunity to demonstrate the glory of God in our own lives, and that by helping those who are in trouble and in pain, we can demonstrate to others the glory of God. It is to show what God is like. How a Christian handles himself in the face of trial, temptation and problems can often be a powerful witness to a watching world.

A few years ago, I saw a close friend of mine in her middle thirties go through a sorrow which none of us can bear to think of, the tragic death of her young husband and father of her two sons. She came through this sorrow very strong, brave, triumphantly, but only through the very close contact and relationship with her God, who is so real to her. What others have done in tragedy, we can do, and the help that they received, we can receive. The world is full of people who can tell us of the supporting power of God.

So suffering is often, in the end, beneficial. It is often character building. We develop physical stamina through hard work, and through suffering we can develop spiritual strength. It changes our perspective and priorities in life. Things that looked so glamorous before, after we have faced a crisis in which we come face to face with the real issues of life, look like mere tinsel or glitter.[9]

"For the Christian, there is always one thing to remember about sorrow and suffering. Christianity does not claim to give the explanation of these things, but it does claim to give the strength to bear them and to even conquer them."[9] Barclay says, "Christianity does not claim to explain the inexplicable, it does give the strength to deal with it."

He gives two ideas which are helpful for us to remember when something happens tragically, beyond our understanding. One is to know that we are not the only ones to whom a thing like this has happened. Paul wrote, "No temptation has overtaken you that is not common to man" (1 Corinthians 10:13). Robert Louis Stevenson was a sick child, and often could not sleep at night. His nurse would pick him up and carry him to the window, and even in the middle of the night, they could see other windows lit up. They would tell each other that in these other houses, there were sick children, who were weary and waiting for the morning to come. Mr. Barclay said, "It is tragic to think of ourselves as the special victim of fate, that our tragedies are unique to ourselves. What happens to us is part of the human situation, and it helps to remember that others, too, are going through the same as we are. We are not lonely sufferers, we are members of a fellowship of suffering, at whose head is Jesus Christ."[10]

Second, we must remember that there are many who not only have gone through this suffering, but who have come through it and who have emerged triumphantly on the other side. There are many, many people who have come through tragedy, pain and sorrow, and who have emerged serene and calm and still able to look at life with steady eyes.

God doesn't promise us that we will be immune to all suffering, but he does promise that to them that love God, all things work together for good. His purpose is to sustain us in the midst of difficulty, rather than to avoid it entirely.

Some of us live our lives as if the chief end in life is our own happiness—free from suffering or anything unpleasant. The worst thing about this goal in life is that it removes God from the center of things.[11] We may not need him as much without problems.

Part of the deceitfulness of sin is that so long as things are going well with us, there is little motivation to give up error and sin. It is when we are hurt and in need that we feel a real need for God. A man who knows no sorrow in his life remains immature, just as a child who knows nothing but total ease in life remains immature. A human father who really loves his child must from time to time cause the child to suffer through discipline. This is not punishment, but rather discipline—so he will grow up to be mature, independent, strong. Without discipline, the child will destroy himself and bring greater suffering on himself by his own blunders. Loving care involves discipline. God is our shepherd who devotedly cares for us, but also guides and restricts his flock for our own safety. He is a Father who disciplines and corrects every son whom he receives.[12]

Suffering and pain are here to stay, for the duration of our lives on earth. Since this is true, why not use it to our own advantage—by concentrating on the inspired word of God, which is able to save our souls and comfort us (1 Peter 1, James 1).[13]

The Bible describes man's existence on the earth as a temporary journey, through which man is prepared for a better and more permanent home in heaven.[14] 2 Corinthians 5:1 says, "For we know that if our earthly house of this tabernacle were dissolved, we have a building of God, a house not made with hands, eternal in the heavens" (KJV). Paul wrote, "For I reckon that the sufferings of this present time are not worthy to be compared with the glory which shall be revealed to us" (Romans 8:18 KJV).

"God has prepared for us a home and he wants us to come to that home. If it were not for the heartache, disappointments and sufferings of this world, we might forget the greater destiny that lies just ahead. The sufferings of this world might have been in part, to cause all of us not to be too satisfied here, but to lift our eyes toward the more wonderful world to come. When we think of the suffering which has come to mankind, we should think of the suffering of Christ, who died that we might live in that world completely free of suffering forever."[15]

Beyond this life with its toils, tears, struggles, disappointments and frustrations lies a world of pure delight of which John wrote in Revelation 21:4. "He will wipe away every tear from their eyes, and death shall be no more, neither shall there be mourning nor crying nor pain any more." What a promise!

"We cannot in this life understand everything, but by the Grace of God, even if we cannot understand, we can *stand*."[16] Ephesians 6:13 tells us, "Therefore take the whole armor of God, that you may be able to withstand in the evil day, and having done all, to stand."

And now, may the Lord bless you and keep you.

References:

The Burden of Pain, Herald of Truth, Batsell Barrett Baxter
None of These Diseases, S. I. McMillen, M.D.
The Problem of Pain, C.S. Lewis

FOR FURTHER STUDY AND DISCUSSION:

1. As Jesus walked among men, do we see him discussing the *"why"* of suffering? Was he not more concerned with alleviating suffering? What does this say to us concerning our own attitude and practice?
2. What is the Christian attitude toward death? Do we communicate this attitude to our children? In what ways?
3. Discuss the wisdom of the following quotations: "We never get enough of an answer on the mystery of suffering if what we are after is an explanation that will satisfy the mind. But there is a talking to God which brings enough of an answer to satisfy the heart."

   "When gripped in adversity's barbed embrace, we may think our deepest need is for an *explanation,* to know *why.* But our deepest need is for *strength,* to know *how*—how adversity may be endured, faced, overcome."

   —Frederick S. Speakman
   The Salty Tang, © 1954
   Fleming A. Revell Co., p. 25

FOOTNOTES:

1. Clovis Chappell, *Questions Jesus Asked* (Nashville: Abingdon Press, renewal 1976), p. 114.
2. Batsell Barrett Baxter, *The Burden of Pain,* sermon from Herald of Truth.
3. Baxter.
4. Baxter.
5. William S. Sadler, *Practice of Psychiatry* (St. Louis: The C.V. Mosby Co., 1953).
6. S.I. McMillan, *None of These Diseases* (Old Tappan, NJ: Fleming H. Revell Co., 1972), p. 64-65.
7. McMillan.
8. Baxter.
9. Baxter.
10. William Barclay
11. Baxter.
12. Baxter.

13. Baxter.
14. Baxter.
15. Baxter.
16. Barclay.

LESSON 12:
Ministry of Love

"If you love those who love you, what credit is that to you?"

Luke 6:32

LESSON SCRIPTURE: Luke 6:32-36   Matthew 5:43-48
OTHER SCRIPTURES: 1 John 4:7-12, 16
                 Romans 5:5
                 1 Corinthians 13:1-7

LOVE—Its Meaning
LOVE—Its Source
LOVE—Its Characteristics
LOVE—Its Reason

by Betty Claunch

"This scripture has been called the central and most famous section of the Sermon on the Mount. It is certainly true that there is no passage in the New Testament which contains such a concentrated expression of the Christian ethic of personal relations as this does. To the ordinary person it describes essential Christianity in action. People who never even go to church know that Jesus said these things and often use this as an excuse to condemn those who profess to be Christians for falling so short of its demands."[1]

Is Jesus demanding the impossible of us? At first glance it would seem that this is true. With what we know about love and the emotions connected with it, it would seem that no one could measure up to this commandment. When we read this passage, we can see that loving those that love us, doing good to those that do good to us, and lending to those from whom we expect to receive, is something that everyone does—that it is nothing out of the ordinary. Christians and non-Christians alike do these things.

But Jesus is saying here that when we have done this, that we have not really done anything. It seems as if he is almost saying,

"So what?" when he says, "What credit is that to you?" Jesus is saying here that he wants his followers to go beyond this kind of love and to love their enemies, do good to those who despitefully use them, and to lend to those from whom they expect to receive nothing in return.

What we want to do in this study is to discuss how this is possible. Can it really be done? How? And why does God want us to love like this?

LOVE—Its Meaning

First, in order to fully understand what Jesus is asking us to do, I think it is important that we understand that here are four Greek words, all with different meanings, that are translated *love* in English. Let us briefly examine the meanings of these words.

"(1) First, there is the noun "storge." This word is characteristic of family love. It is the word used to describe the love of a parent for a child or a child for a parent. In other words, it is family affection.

"(2) Then, there is the word "eros." This word describes the love of a man for a maid. There is always passion in it. Eros has been described as the terrible longing. There is nothing essentially bad in this word—it simply describes the passion of human love. But as time went on, it began to be tinged with the idea of lust, rather than love, and it never occurs in the New Testament.

"(3) Then there is "philia," which is the warmest and best Greek word for love. It describes real love, real affection. It is the highest kind of love. The present participle is the word which describes a man's closest and nearest and dearest friends.

"(4) Then there is "agape," which is the word used in this passage. The real meaning of "agape" is *unconquerable benevolence, INVINCIBLE GOOD WILL.* "Agapan," the verb, describes the active feeling of benevolence toward the other person. If we regard a person with "agape," it means that no matter what that person does to us, no matter how he treats us, no matter if he insults, injures or grieves us, we will not feel bitterness in our hearts for him, but will regard him with that unconquerable benevolence and goodwill which will seek nothing but his highest good."[2]

The Agape is the love that reaches out to all mankind, irrespective of class, creed, nationality or circumstance. It recognizes all men as the common offspring of God. As James M. Tolle described it in *The Christian Graces,* "It is the love we are to have for men, not because of any pleasure they may afford us, not because we like them or agree with them, but because they are *men,* human beings, made in the image of God."[3]

From loving people in this way, I think there are some things that we need to realize.

"Jesus never asked us to love our enemies in the same way we love our nearest and dearest. The very word is different. To love our enemies in the same way we love those who are nearest to us would neither be possible nor right. It is an entirely different kind of love. What is the difference then? In the case of our nearest and dearest, we can't help loving them. We talk about 'falling in love.' It is something that comes to us quite unsought. But in the case of our enemies, love is *not* only something of the heart; it is something of the *will*. It is not something which we cannot help—it is something which we have to will ourselves into doing. It is, in fact, a victory and a conquest over that which comes instinctively to the natural man. It means a determination of the mind whereby we achieve this unconquerable good will, even to those who hurt and injure us. Agape, someone has said, is the power to love those whom we do not like and who do not like us. In fact, we can only have agape when Jesus Christ enables us to conquer our natural tendency to anger and to bitterness and to achieve this invincible goodwill to all men.

"This brings us to one of the most important parts of the lesson. *This is a commandment that is only possible for a Christian.* Only the grace of Jesus Christ and the love of God can enable a person to have this kind of love in his personal relationships with other people. It is only when Christ lives in our hearts that this bitterness will die and this kind of love come to life."[4]

LOVE—Its Source

God is love and only by having God's love in us can we love as God loved. Listen to John, in 1 John 4:7-12, 16: "Beloved, let us love one another; for love is of God, and he who loves is born of God and knows God. He who does not love does not know God; for God is love. In this the love of God was made manifest among us, that God sent his only Son into the world, so that we might live through him. In this is love, not that we loved God but that he loved us and sent his Son to be the expiation for our sins. Beloved, if God so loved us, we also ought to love one another. No man has ever seen God; if we love one another, God abides in us and his love is perfected in us . . . So we know and believe the love God has for us. God is love, and he who abides in love abides in God, and God abides in him."

Before we can love others, we must be able to accept the fact that God loves us unconditionally. He does not love us because we are lovable, because of anything we have done or because we deserve to be loved. Paul said, in Romans 5, that Christ died for us while we were sinners, and he also said that we were reconciled to God while we were still enemies. Christ did not die for us because of anything that we had done or because we deserved it. He died for us because he loved us.

The big question, then, is *how do we get this love of God in our hearts?* Paul said in Romans 5:5 that the love of God is shed abroad in our hearts by the Holy Spirit. Has God promised to give his Holy Spirit to everyone? The answer is yes, but there are conditions.

Believers on the Day of Pentecost, about whom we read in Acts 2, were told by Peter to repent and be baptized and they would receive the gift of the Holy Spirit. He said, "The promise is to you and your children and to all that are far off, every one whom the Lord our God calls to him" (Acts 2:39). This promise is directed as much to me today as it was to those people then, *but* it is only when a person submits his life to Christ and is willing to be obedient to him that the Spirit of God comes to dwell in his life, bringing that unselfish love of God.

"When Christ comes into the human heart, He brings His grace to transform our natural love, sometimes poor and shriveled and easily quenched, into His perfect love . . . . No doubt progress will be slow, but if there is anything genuine in our commitment to Christ, *it will come.*"[5]

Maybe, if we are not able to love everyone in this unselfish way, we should ask ourselves the question, "How really genuine and total is my commitment?"

LOVE—Its Characteristics

This love that we are talking about is not a *passive* feeling of benevolence and goodwill to people. It is an *active* feeling of benevolence and goodwill. It is something to do. The Bible does not speak of Christian love as an emotion. It tells us what love does. Jesus told his disciples that their love would be demonstrated by keeping his commandments. In 1 Corinthians 13, Paul describes what love does and does not do; he also warns that anything we do, even something seemingly grand or spectacular, is worth nothing if not motivated by love.

Now this love makes a *vast* difference in our lives. "God cannot hide springtime in the heart of an apple tree and trust the tree to keep the secret. It will proclaim it to the world in tender green, in blossoms of beauty, and at last in delicious fruit. Even so, when love comes into our hearts, it expresses itself in many ways."[6] As Paul shows, it makes us patient and kind, not jealous, or conceited, or proud or selfish, or irritable. This familiar chapter can serve as a daily reminder of love's characteristics.

LOVE—Its Reason

Why does God want us to have this kind of love?

"The answer is very simple and very tremendous. It is that such love makes a man like God. The action of God in the world is one of benevolence—He makes his sun to rise on the good and the evil; He sends his rain on the just and the unjust. Even the Jews were impressed with the sheer benevolence of God to saint and sinner alike. In God there is this universal benevolence, even toward men who have broken his law and broken his heart.

"Jesus says that we must have this love so that we may become sons of our Father who is in heaven. The reason for God wanting us to have it is that he has it, and if we have it, we become nothing less than sons of God or Godlike men.

"Here I think we have the key to one of the most difficult sentences in the New Testament. 'Be ye therefore perfect, as your Father is perfect.' On the face of it, that sounds like a commandment which could not possibly have anything to do with us. There is not a one of us who would even faintly connect ourselves with perfection as we think of perfection. The Greek word for perfect is 'teleios,' and it is often used in a very special way, and it has nothing to do with what we may call absolute perfection. The Greek idea of perfection is functional. A thing is 'teleios' if it realizes the purpose for which it was planned; a man is 'teleios' or perfect if he realizes the purpose for which he was created and sent into the world. Then, for what purpose was man created? The Bible leaves us in no doubt as to that. In the beginning, in the creation, we find God saying, "Let us make man in our image and after our likeness." Man was created to be like God. The characteristic of God is the universal benevolence, this unconquerable goodwill, this constant seeking of the highest good of every man. God loves saint and sinner alike, and no matter what men do to Him, He seeks nothing but their highest good.

"It is the whole teaching of the Bible that we only reach our manhood by becoming godlike. The one thing which makes us like God is the *love* that never ceases to care for men, no matter what men do to it. We realize our manhood, we enter upon Christian perfection, when we learn to forgive as God forgives, and to love as God loves."[7]

Father, we thank you for your unselfish love for us. We pray that each one of us will totally submit our lives to you to the extent that your Spirit will live in our hearts, bringing your wonderful love, helping us to love all men. Amen.

—Betty Claunch

LOVE—Its Practice

"*We can begin to learn love by practicing.* There it is in black and white. Once we have caught on to something of the nature of God's love operative in us, we can begin to use it creatively only by practice. God designed our minds to function best through regular exercise of our wills. If we practice love, we become loving. If we practice hate, we become hateful. We choose the nature of our exercise. Only the overly sentimental person goes about with his head in a bag believing that all people are selfish at heart. Christian love is never sentimentalized love; it is always realistic."[8]

How, then, do we learn to love? Here are some suggestions:

1. Practice the love you have—practice until it becomes a habit. If your love for someone is weak—*act* toward them with love. To act constantly as if you cared is almost surely to come to care, because we love those for whom we sacrifice. We may also find that our acts of kindness work a change in the conduct of the one on whom we bestow them. Have you ever thought, "I believe she really likes me"? If so, what happens? More than likely, you begin to like her.

2. Learn to love yourself properly. Our love for ourselves must not take the form of conceit or arrogance. Neither does proper love for self necessarily mean that we like ourselves, but that we wish our own good. Many of us do not like ourselves, but if we begin to love ourselves with 'agape,' God-love, we may end up liking ourselves. This kind of love includes practical concern for our own well-being, such as rest, exercise, and balanced diet—*not* self-indulgence or over-indulgence. Unconcern for these requirements of our physical body shows a lack of love for those who love and depend on us. Love of self also means a recognition of our own individual potentials in God's sight. One who is constantly minimizing her ability or potential, either to herself or others, is not humble, but lacks proper self-love.

3. Think on the love of God for you and the love of others for you. Exercise the mind with loving thoughts. "Fill your mind with those things that are good and deserve praise: things that are true, noble, right, pure, lovely, and honorable" (Philippians 4:8 TEV).

4. Never forget the source of your love. "By surrendering to Jesus, we are reborn. Being reborn, we love. The surest of all sure ways of loving is to let into your heart him whose nature and whose name is love.

The unloved man is pitiable, but the man who loves nobody is more pitiable still. Of all the privileges that we have, there is none higher than the privilege of loving. Nobody ever loved anybody too well, although we may have loved God too little. "In the matter of loving," Dr. Chappell has said, "you can let yourself go, for the more you love the more like God you become."[9]

SUGGESTION FOR FURTHER STUDY AND DISCUSSION:

Divide the class into three groups to discuss practical application of 1 Corinthians 13:1-7. Questions are provided to stimulate thinking. If time permits, the class may reassemble and report from each group.

GROUP I (verses 1-3)

1. Discuss the ways in which love may be a universal language.
2. Which would you rather have as a teacher of your class—an eloquent speaker or one who can convey in simple language and in class discussions a love which she demonstrates in her life. Discuss.
3. Is self-sacrifice done for motives other than love? If so, what? What good is self-sacrifice if it turns to self-pity?

GROUP II (verses 4-5)

1. Is it possible to be any of these (impatient, unkind, rude, etc.) and still be a loving person? What do we work on—loving the person or being patient?
2. What part does self-love play? Why? How?
3. In practicing love, how do we both "let your light shine before men" and "do not let the left hand know what the right hand is doing"?

GROUP III (verses 6-7)

1. Is it possible to look for the best in *everyone*? Discuss the results of such an attitude.
2. Is it naive to expect the best of people?

FOOTNOTES:

1. William Barclay, *The Gospel of Matthew, Vol. 1* (Philadelphia: Westminster Press), p. 171.
2. Barclay, p. 171.
3. James M. Tolle, *The Christian Graces* (Beaumont, TX: Tolle Publications, 1965), p. 63.
4. Barclay, pp. 172-174.
5. Eileen Guden, *To Live in Love* (Grand Rapids, MI: Zondervan Publishing House, 1967), p. 109.
6. Clovis Chappell, *Sermons on Simon Peter* (Nashville: Abingdon Press, 1959), pp. 110-111.
7. Barclay, pp. 174-176.

8. Eugenia Price, *Make Love Your Aim* (Grand Rapids, MI: Zondervan Publishing House, 1967), pp. 84-85.
9. Chappell, p. 115.

LESSON 13:
Power of God

"Is not this why you are wrong, that you know neither the scriptures nor the power of God?"
Mark 12:24

LESSON SCRIPTURE: Mark 12:18-25
OTHER SCRIPTURES: 2 Corinthians 4:18   Ephesians 1:18-20
John 1:11-13   Ephesians 3:14-21

It seems to be a rather ridiculous riddle with which the Sadducees confronted Jesus. Can you imagine seven brothers successively marrying one woman? Even based on a Mosaic Law that a man should marry his brother's widow and raise children to his name, the idea of *seven* doing so is a little farfetched in our way of thinking. The punch line comes with a humorous twist, "In the resurrection, whose wife will she be?"

The question which the Sadducees put to Jesus had been well planned; their object was certainly not serious argument, but the more dangerous weapon of ridicule. Their subject was the resurrection, making their question very hypocritical in that they asked about a resurrection in which they did not believe. Their intention was not to find out anything about the resurrection, but to illustrate at Jesus' expense how absurd was the belief in any such doctrine.[1]

Indeed, in those days it was a difficult doctrine to defend as it was not yet a matter of hope or faith. The passages in the Old Testament on the subject of the "hereafter" were not very clear, and the grand fact of history—the resurrection of Christ—had not yet taken place. Also, the beliefs of the Pharisees on the subject had deprived the resurrection of its grand majesty and had surrounded it with fresh difficulties.

For instance, it would be hard to imagine that, even in the state of scientific knowledge of the times, anyone could have really

111

believed that there was a small bone in the spine which was indestructible and from this the new man would spring. Even more strange was the idea that all Israel should rise on Palestinian soil; thus, there were cavities underground in which the body would roll till it reached the Holy Land, there to arise to newness of life. Whether a person would rise in his clothes was a point of discussion, and it was assumed from 1 Samuel 28:14 that the risen body would look exactly as in life. The doctrine of the resurrection was so laden with realistic ideas and legends that it is easy to see why the Sadducees rejected it. Their question of whose wife the woman who had been successively married to seven brothers would be was based on this grossly *materialistic view* of the Pharisees.[2]

But in the view of Christ the resurrection would be very different from all this and would occupy a place of prominence, as it was the climax of His mission, toward which He daily journeyed, and the core of that "good news" that was to be preached to the world. But Jesus could not have spoken such thought to the Sadducees; even His disciples did not understand at this time. Instead, He answered seriously, in words they all could understand, appealing to the *Word* and to the *Power of God*—how God *has* manifested Himself, and how He *will* Manifest Himself—the one flowing from the other. The basis of faith in the resurrection is faith in the power of God, which is far greater than man's concept of joy and hope might suppose. Jesus further implied that human relationships will be superceded; by saying, "they are like angels," He showed that life after death cannot be described in words bound to earthly images.

The question becomes irrelevant when the eternal world is viewed as spiritual and immaterial. What the religious people of Jesus' day needed to realize and what we need to be assured of is that God's power will work, not a mere re-awakening, but a transformation. The power of God will transform this present body of sin and corruption. All of earth that is in us will be left behind, and all of God and goodness will be fully-developed and ripened into perfect beauty.[3]

Thus Jesus silenced the Sadducees, astonished the multitude, and even drew praise from the scribes for His answer. What was His answer? Rhetorically, Jesus Himself countered with a question: "Is not this why you are wrong, that you know neither the scriptures, nor the power of God?" In what was Jesus accusing them to be wrong? Were they wrong in that their question assumed the fact of a resurrection? No, because the resurrection is a fact. Were they wrong in believing in a resurrection themselves? No, because we know that they did not believe. Then what?

I suggest to you that what Jesus was challenging and what he was attacking in them was their false sense of reality; for the question they posed showed an earthly concept of what is to be a spiritual resurrection. Perhaps Jesus is saying to them, in essence, "Isn't this part of your problem—that you have such a limited view of what constitutes reality?"

Could Jesus be asking me this question? As I reflect on this thought, it seems to me that one of the biggest problems in remaining committed daily and experiencing the abundant life is that it is so easy to lose the reality of my Christian life—the physical tends to overwhelm the spiritual. For our generation is extremely naturalistic and almost totally committed to the concept of the natural causes of our world operating in a closed system. Because of this we see some people who reject Christianity, as they cannot accept the spiritual and the supernatural ideas it presents. We see some religious people who may claim to be Christians but who deny the virgin birth, the miracles, the resurrection. There are even those who have gone to the other extreme and embraced the mysticism of the east, perhaps in rebellion against this naturalistic concept which is so prevalent in our world. Even though we may be Bible-believing Christians, if we are not careful, this naturalism of our generation tends to creep in upon us, and before we know it, we begin to lose the reality of our Christian lives.

We *must* understand that the universe is not what our generation says it is, seeing only the naturalistic universe; and we must constantly keep in mind the Biblical view of the universe. Francis Schaeffer, in his book "True Spirituality," likens this biblical view of the natural and the supernatural existing together to make up the whole of reality of two halves of an orange. As neither half is the whole orange, in the same way neither the natural nor the supernatural (call them "physical" and "spiritual" if you like) is the whole of reality, but one flows into the other. This is an important point, as there is a tendency to think of the natural and physical as "now" and the supernatural and spiritual as "hereafter," thus robbing my Christian life in this world of its meaning and power. In using the word "supernatural" let us be careful to give its biblical meaning and not to be thinking of the fairy tales, folklore, and mysticism with which men have surrounded it. According to the Bible, the natural is what is normally seen; the supernatural is what is normally unseen—"We look not to the things that are seen but to the things that are unseen; for the things that are seen are transient, but the things that are unseen are eternal" (2 Corinthians 4:18). When speaking of the supernatural or spiritual, we are speaking of things normally unseen, about which the Bible teaches.

We may illustrate by looking to the incident in Jesus' life when He took the inner core of His disciples up to the mountain and, as there appeared with Him Moses and Elijah, a voice from heaven said, "This is my beloved Son, hear Him!" While this was taking place, the other disciples had been left at the foot of the mountain;

the crowd was still there, and physical life was going on as usual. The supernatural and the natural were happening at the same time, existing together. Of course, we know that this was a unique event, the turning point of the ministry of Jesus and a very important means of establishing His credibility. It's not the sort of thing God has promised that we will experience. However, the Bible does, in many places, promise the existence of the spiritual—the unseen—to us. For instance, we are told that when a sinner repents the angels in heaven rejoice. I wonder if, when a sinner does repent and obeys Christ in baptism, our minds are fixed on the fact that at that very moment the angels are rejoicing; and also, as this one goes down into the water and comes up out of the water, he is being born again. This is something that you and I can not physically see, but we know, by faith, that it is true. Doesn't this show that God considers both halves of reality important to His creatures in that He commanded us to go through this physical act of obedience? Some religious people contend that baptism is unimportant—why be dipped in water? Perhaps God sees that the natural and physical things we as mortals live with are so much a part of us that the combination of a physical burial and a spiritual rebirth (the two halves of reality) make this *very real* and important to us.

Imagine with me two chairs. One is labeled "Faith," the other "Unfaith." Schaeffer suggests, also, that everyone (depending on how he views reality) sits in one of these two chairs, so to speak. There are those who have only the naturalistic viewpoint, who deny the supernatural—they sit in a chair labeled "unfaith" and interpret truth against that background. Those who embrace both halves of reality sit in the chair labeled "faith" and interpret truth accordingly. Those of us who are Christians look at the person sitting in the chair of "unfaith" and say, "How sad, for they are missing what life is all about!" What shall we say of one who sits in the chair of "faith" but lives as though only the physical were real? Shall we not also say, "How sad!" I'm afraid that we Christians do this all too often, and perhaps that is why many people, both within and without the church, are dissatisfied with life and feel they are missing what they want. To just believe in both halves of reality is not enough. Victory as a Christian can come only as we actually *live* this reality; as we come to realize that Christ as the bridegroom, by the indwelling spirit (unseen), works in us as the bride, by our faith and obedience (seen), to produce the fruits of the spirit. Looking at the two halves of reality, this is no longer such an amazing doctrine, and we can begin to realize the terrific power of God working in our lives.[4]

No longer need our age of materialism leave us confused as to what is real and what is of value. No longer need Jesus say to us, "Isn't a false sense of reality part of your problem?"

He went on to ask the Sadducees on this occasion, "Isn't part of your problem the fact that you do not know the Scriptures?" Is this our problem? Sometimes we pride ourselves on Bible study and on knowing the Scriptures and the will of God; but this is certainly unjustifiable, as there is no limit to the gain from studying God's word, no point of having arrived, of having all knowledge. Let us never minimize the value of Bible study, and let us combine our study with earnest and sincere prayer for understanding of what we read in the Bible, and for wisdom and guidance in living it. For, in many situations, even though we know what God's word says, we are still faced with the tedious task of sorting and pinpointing just what is the proper action or what is the real value. For this further guidance God has given the avenue of prayer, and there are wells of wisdom to be gained through its power.

The ever changing values in the world about us can deceive the heart that is not filled with God's love and wisdom. Amid today's confusion about reality and true values, we need to be constantly impressing the spiritual on our minds; there is no better way than through prayer. Is it not true that when we pray earnestly for one who is sick, we deepen our compassion; each time we offer a sincere petition for someone in need, we are more benevolent; and as we plead for wisdom and guidance in a particular situation, it becomes easier to surrender our will to His. And as we pray daily, we may begin to find his peace abiding with us, for we are experiencing the release of trusting the one who has all power![5]

What is this power? Do you know the power of God? Jesus told the Sadducees that they did not know this power. One of the saddest sentences written is found in John 1:11, "He came unto his own, and his own received him not" (KJV). But there were those who did receive him, and that sad sentence is followed by one of the most thrilling: "But to all who received him . . . he gave power to become children of God." That is what Jesus is constantly doing for those who receive him—giving power to become new creatures in Christ, power to become *sons of God* (Romans 8:14-16)!

What does it mean to become a SON OF GOD? Far more, we can be assured, than to be a creation of God only. What one creates is something he makes, which is different from himself. Man is created in God's image, to be sure, but he does not have the kind of life God has—eternal life. We can see this analysis in the fact that what man creates is not man—it may be a building, a painting, a statue. If a man is a clever enough carver, he may make a statue which looks very much like a man, but, of course, it is not a real man; it cannot breathe or think, is not alive. A man who changed from his God-created natural or biological life would have gone through as big a change as a statue which changed from being carved stone to being a real man. Is the world a great sculptor's shop, we are statues, and some day we will come to life?[6]

Consider what Paul says in Romans 8:19: "The whole creation is on tiptoe to see the wonderful sight of the sons of God coming into their own. The world of creation cannot as yet see reality, not because it chooses to be blind, but because in God's purpose it has been limited—yet it has been given hope" (Phillips Modern English).

The fact that we, as Christians, are sons of God means we see in the two halves of reality, not as just something that takes place when we reach heaven (of course, we will realize its culmination only then), but as something that has its beginning *now*. We now have the spirit as a guarantee of this assurance, for we read in Romans 8:16 that "it is the spirit himself bearing witness with our spirit that we are children of God." Thus, the power to become sons, or children of God is power to *live*—power to live, not only in the hereafter, but power to live now! We can begin to know "the immeasurable greatness of his power in us who believe" (Ephesians 1:19). I urge every Christian to read, study, even gloat, in the teachings in God's Word that tell us something of His power and that offer promises—precious promises—to us. Do we realize that God promises us power to be patient, to endure, to be strong, even to overflow with hope? How much consolation is it to know that "God is able to make all grace abound to you, so that in all things at all times, having all that you need, you will abound in every good work" (2 Corinthians 9:8 NIV)?

Our God is *able:*

—to change our lowly body to be like his glorious body (Philippians 3:21).
—to provide every blessing in abundance (2 Corinthians 9:8).
—to guard the soul's treasure (2 Timothy 1:12).
—to save those who draw near to God through Jesus (Hebrews 7:25).
—to keep you from falling and to present you without blemish before the presence of glory (Jude 24).
—to do far more abundantly than all that we ask, or think, *by the power at work within us* (Ephesians 3:20).

God promises us power:

—to become sons of God (John 1:12, 13).
—to endure, to be patient (Colossians 1:11).
—to be strong (Ephesians 6:10).
—to overflow with hope (Romans 15:13).
—to know the immeasurable greatness of his power in us (Ephesians 1:18, 19).

—to know all things that pertain to life and godliness (2 Peter 1:3).
—to comprehend the breadth, length, height, depth (Ephesians 3:18).
—to know the love of God (Ephesians 3:19).
—to be filled with the fullness of God (Ephesians 3:19).

"I have laid up thy word in my heart, that I might not sin against thee," (Psalm 119:11) is an example to emulate. In Hebrews 4:12, we have this assurance: "the word of God is living and active (quick and powerful—KJV)." If we lay up these powerful words in our heart, draw on their precious promises and trust God for power to live, surely victory will be ours! Listen to Ephesians 1:18-20 in the Phillips translation:

That you may receive that inner illumination of the spirit which will make you realize how great is the hope to which he is calling you—the magnificence and splendor of the inheritance promised to Christians—and *how tremendous is the power available to us who believe in God.* That power is the same divine energy which was demonstrated in Christ when he raised him from the dead and gave him the place of supreme honor in Heaven. . . .

Power to live is what we need. It is no good talking about assessing values unless we *live* them! And living such values as we have studied in this course is an impossibility for me on my own—I need all the help I can get! My problem, and no doubt your problem, is not in understanding what is of true value, but in letting my life be an example of that value. I can easily see that the teachings of Jesus uphold an ethic far superior to any other that I know, but also far superior to anything I can live up to under my own power.

"The teachings of Jesus happen to be the most serious judgment ever pronounced on the way we humans live. They happen to be the most crushing indictment of our boastful human successes, the most relentless and abrupt stripping away from the chest of our pride, of all our precious medals in the fine art of living that the human spirit has or will encounter."[7]

Surely these teachings of Jesus are not just idealistic dreaming nor a command to do the impossible. There is a major secret to this Christianity. It is a faith that, in and of ourselves, we cannot live up to. But the secret is that even though we can't, yet we know we must. Even when we are desperately certain that life is solved only as we do live up to it, we still know that, in and of ourselves alone, we can't. But we keep trying, and the reason we do is the hope God has placed within us. Paul says this secret is "Christ in you, the hope of glory" (Colossians 1:27). Because we have this hope and

God's power to help us to live, we keep trying. We turn to God and say, "God I keep bungling, I keep falling. Will you help me live these values? Help me know what is best in every situation, and not only to know but also to *do* what is best. Complete in me all these dreams of yours, and make me into your image."

Thank God for His power! We have His promises that through the inner illumination of the spirit we can be radiant and overflowing with energy, joy, wisdom and love so as to reflect back to God something of His own power and goodness. We have confidence to live because of our faith in His indwelling spirit that is working through us to work the works that God has put us here to accomplish according to His purpose. We can then claim the prayer of Paul's in Ephesians 3:16-21:

> I pray that out of his glorious riches he may strengthen you with POWER through his Spirit in your inner being, so that Christ may dwell in your hearts through faith. And I pray that you, being rooted and established in love, may have POWER, together with the saints, to grasp how wide and long and high and deep is the love of Christ, and to know this love that surpasses knowledge—that you may be filled to the measure of all the fullness of God.

> Now to him who is able to do immeasurably more than all we ask or imagine, according to his POWER that is at work within us, to him be glory in the church and in Christ Jesus throughout all generations, for ever and ever! Amen (NIV).

FOR FURTHER STUDY AND DISCUSSION:

Discuss the Scriptures given under *God is able,* and *God promises us power,* giving special attention to practical applications.

FOOTNOTES:

1. *Broadman Bible Commentary, Vol. 9* (Nashville: Broadman Press), pp. 364-365.
2. Alfred Edersheim, *Life and Times of Jesus, the Messiah, Vol. 2* (Grand Rapids, MI: Eerdman's Publishing Co.), pp. 369, 399.
3. Edersheim, pp. 401-402.
4. Francis Schaeffer, *True Spirituality* (Wheaton, IL: Tyndale House Publishers), pp. 62-64.
5. Della Howell, "Prayer Sets Values Straight," *Christian Woman,* April 1968.
6. C.S. Lewis, *Beyond Personality* (New York: MacMillan Co.), pp. 5-7.
7. Frederick B. Speakman, *The Salty Tang* (Old Tappan, NJ: Fleming H. Revell Co., 1954), p. 111.

APPLYING the "two halves of reality" in review:

We began this course with the suggestion that it might be well that we take inventory and re-evaluate our values. The word "value" is defined as the *real* worth of something. Then we might ask ourselves: "In view of reality, as presented in this last lesson, what is this worth? What is its value?" If this is used as a method of assessing values, then it follows:

KNOWING GOD PERSONALLY becomes a thing of high value because it can be very real. God is supernatural and unseen. Yet He exists along with the natural and is interested and concerned with every aspect of my physical life. To know God personally becomes a high value because of the relationship of the daily, hourly, moment by moment influence on all my physical activities. When we realize God's presence as a certain fact always, no longer need we have vague misconceptions of our relations with Him. Then he is with us always; words spoken in prayer are as really spoken to him as if our eyes could see Him and our hands could touch him.

In the same way, the PRESENCE OF JESUS is real, just as your presence is real; and the PEACE He brings because He promised it has a drastic effect on my actions in the flesh.

SEEKING GLORY from one another and not from God is humanism—only one half of the orange. Viewed from both sides of reality, seeking glory from God includes proper approval of fellowmen. "As far as it depends on you, live at peace with everyone" (Romans 12:18 NIV). "He who thus serves Christ is acceptable to God and approved by men" (Romans 14:18).

My use of MATERIAL THINGS becomes less of a dilemma and more of a joy as I see the two halves of reality. God grants material blessings because He is interested in *all* our needs, even bread. Bread is God's gift; thus our use of daily bread brings a sense of God into our daily lives. Material things seen *only* as material things have no real value except to sustain physical life. Material things accumulated for material value become idolatry and a negative value in that they pose a threat of danger of one's being possessed by them and losing the soul because of them. But material things *used,* in a life devoted to God's glory, combine the two halves of reality and become a real value (See Ephesians 4:28).

As for SUFFERING, Paul considered well both realities when he said in Romans 8: "I consider that the sufferings of this present time are not worth comparing with the glory that is to be revealed to us."

The FAMILY RELATIONSHIPS which the church, the body of Christ, offers me become of priceless value when I see my brothers and sisters as people who have feelings like mine, who have problems and faults and talents—but who have also the same all-loving Father and the same cleansing blood (a blood-kin) and the same indwelling spirit.

That "agape" LOVE, the God-like love which has been poured out into my heart can produce fruit *only* as I begin to see people (*every* person) in the light of both realities—a human being with human needs, but more than that, one whose soul is worth more than all the world.

The two realities, you can see, are not opposing but blending. They make up the whole—the ONENESS of living.

THERE ARE NO LONGER MANY VALUES, ONLY ONE, THE WILL OF OUR FATHER IN HEAVEN.